Heather,
With Best
Regards,

Praise for *Make Room for Her*

"*Make Room for Her* expertly guides the reader through a changing business environment and effectively builds out an exciting new leadership model that should be adopted by organizations seeking to reassess their commitment to the advancement of women in leadership and effectively move the needle to garner stronger results."
—*Paul LaPiana, Senior Vice President, MetLife*

"*Make Room for Her* in its title and in every paragraph delivers the essential message of Integrated Leadership to leaders at every level of every organization in all three sectors. This new and indispensable handbook delivers a new model for the organization of the future."
—*Frances Hesselbein, President and CEO,*
The Frances Hesselbein Leadership Institute

"Rebecca Shambaugh's extremely informative, entertaining, and insightful new book, *Make Room for Her*, is aimed at both a male and female audience. It succinctly describes business leadership models that drive top performance in organizations, as well as proactive steps female executives can take to assume responsibility for their careers and become a significant part of the leadership equation."
—*Karen Bechtel, Managing Director, The Carlyle Group*

"Diversity is about more than values and culture—it's also about taking action. Shambaugh provides a road map to cultural change with practical stops along the way for employees of both genders."
—*Sylvia Ann Hewlett, Economist and CEO,*
Center for Talent Innovation

"Make room to read Rebecca Shambaugh's new book on Integrated Leadership. It will cause you to rethink the leadership model your organization follows and provide you with clear strategies for integrating the best of both men and women leaders to drive performance."

—*Dottie Brienza, Chief Diversity Officer and Executive Talent Leader, Merck*

"In today's dynamic marketplace, every business needs a diversity of ideas and new perspectives to help them solve problems and seize opportunities. Actively sponsoring women for leadership opportunities is more than just the right thing to do—it's an essential part of winning the best talent and building a competitive edge. Rebecca Shambaugh's years of strategic leadership development, her extensive study of current business trends, and her real-world interactions with industry leaders have given her extraordinary insight into the importance of increasing women's senior leadership roles."

—*John B. Veihmeyer, Chairman and Chief Executive Officer, KPMG LLP*

MAKE ROOM FOR HER

WHY COMPANIES NEED AN INTEGRATED LEADERSHIP MODEL TO ACHIEVE EXTRAORDINARY RESULTS

REBECCA SHAMBAUGH

New York   Chicago   San Francisco   Lisbon   London   Madrid   Mexico City
Milan   New Delhi   San Juan   Seoul   Singapore   Sydney   Toronto

The **McGraw·Hill** Companies

1 2 3 4 5 6 7 8 9 10   QFR/QFR   1 8 7 6 5 4 3 2

ISBN 978-0-07-179792-4
MHID 0-07-179792-0

e-ISBN 978-0-07-179793-1
e-MHID 0-07-179793-9

Library of Congress Cataloging-in-Publication Data
Shambaugh, Rebecca.
    Make room for her : why companies need an integrated leadership model to achieve extraordinary results / by Rebecca Shambaugh.
        p. cm.
    ISBN 978-0-07-149792-4 (alk. paper) — ISBN 978-0-07-179792-0 (alk. paper) 1. Leadership.   2. Women exectuives.   3. Leadership in women.   4. Sex discrimination.   I. Title.
    HD57.7S4752   2013
    658.4'092—dc23
                                                            2012034104

McGraw-Hill books are available at special quantity discounts to use as premiums and sales promotions or for use in corporate training programs. To contact a representative, please e-mail us at bulksales@mcgraw-hill.com.

This book is printed on acid-free paper.

Contents

v

Part II

Integrated Leadership: Men's Role

Part III

Integrated Leadership: Women's Role

Part IV

Integrated Leadership:
The Organization's Role

Introduction

HAVING SERVED as an executive for three Fortune 500 companies and running my own leadership development company for the past 20 years, I feel qualified to say that the one constant in business is change! But even though constant change has become the norm, I am amazed at the tremendous impact it still has on all of us. Never before have I seen so many business leaders, across all business sectors and industries, work so hard to juggle so many challenges and opportunities. Shifting market conditions, higher customer expectations, ever-evolving workforce demographics, new business processes, constant advances in technology, and rapid social changes are causing many business leaders to rethink the kind of leadership that is needed to be successful now and in the future.

Furthermore, many futurists have said that our world is in a time of dramatic change and that we will continue to experience unresolved complexities that will call for all of us to adapt to a new way of thinking and leading—one that does not fight the new realities but adapts and flows with the new external forces that are impacting us today.

All this evidence indicates that we are on the brink of a significant change in how we lead our organizations. What we need is a sustainable approach for developing the best leadership for success in today's economy. *Integrated Leadership* harnesses the collective human intelligence available to us on gender-balanced teams. There's strength in each gender, just as there's strength in a diversity of life experiences, age experiences, racial experiences, ethnicity, culture, and so many other aspects of life that make us who we are.

If the issue of leadership is important to you—as an executive trying to develop the next generation of leaders, a leader wanting to
improve your team's effectiveness, or someone looking to join the
ranks of leadership in your organization—this book is for you. While
it addresses the lack of women in senior leadership, let me be clear that
it is not a book about the need for diversity or the need to do a better
job of promoting women. Nor is it another self-help book for women
in business. In fact, many of these types of books are based on the
premise that the reason women are not advancing is that the system
is stacked against them or there is something wrong with the system.
I disagree.

I have been an advocate for more women in the corporate leadership ranks for more than two decades now. I have spoken on this subject at over 100 conferences worldwide, worked with Fortune 500
companies as well as nonprofit organizations, and coached both men
and women in senior leadership positions about how to attract, retain,
and develop women leaders to enhance the competitive advantage and
profitability of their organization both now and in the future. I believe
it's time for women to assume responsibility for their own career
advancement and adapt their beliefs, assumptions, and behaviors
accordingly. They must learn to tap into their own power, identify the
patterns that keep them from moving forward, and take responsibility for their success.

This book changes the conversation from advancing women to
leveraging gender intelligence and together driving better results. It
makes the business case for having a balance of men and women at
senior levels of leadership. Consequently, the book is as relevant to
male leaders as it is to female leaders. It encourages and enables both
men's and women's active participation in the process of creating Integrated Leadership. It focuses on women, not only on what they can do
to advance, but just as important, on what male leaders can do to foster a better balance of leadership perspective that yields better business

results. It incorporates the male perspective and advice on how women can grow and advance into senior leadership roles, as well as the female perspective on how men can best coach and support them in doing so.

In today's fast-paced environment, business leaders are looking for concrete advice. This book goes beyond concept and theory and provides a detailed plan for building Integrated Leadership teams in your organization, including:

- Assessments for deepening awareness and prioritizing development
- Gender-specific advice, tools, and techniques
- Interesting case studies based on my work coaching hundreds of women and men leaders
- Interviews with more than 50 successful top executives

Today's marketplace is calling for a new approach to leadership. Integrated Leadership is the key to capturing and maintaining a lasting competitive advantage.

Part I

Integrated Leadership:
How Men and Women
Can Achieve Extraordinary
Results Together

Chapter 1

The Need for Integrated Leadership

Not long ago, I sat down over coffee with the CEO of an IT company. The CEO—we'll call him Robert—shared with me that his organization had been the market leader in its industry for the past five years and had enjoyed consistent growth and profitability. The company's success to that point, he believed, was based on its leadership and its employees' sheer drive and relentless focus on key results.

Yet despite its past success, Robert confided that he had deep concerns about the company's future. A competitor with a creative, new technology had recently overtaken Robert's company as the market leader, and he had just learned that his company had lost one of its key customers to this competitor. To make matters worse, the organization's most recent employee survey revealed that morale was low, people were burned out, communication was lacking, and employees had lost faith in leadership.

In strategy sessions with his executive team, Robert had sat and listened as various leaders rationalized that the competitor's innovation was nothing more than a fad that would quickly run its course, and when that happened, customers would come back. Robert shared, "That was when it hit me that this was the kind of thinking that got us where we are today . . . in trouble. Looking around the table, I realized that I have a team full of left-brain thinkers who are proficient in fact-based decision making, efficiency and process oriented, and extremely results focused. But we are sorely missing creativity, collaboration, a big-picture perspective, listening skills, and emotional intelligence. When our big customer left for the competition, they told us that they felt we didn't listen to or understand their needs."

Then Robert told me about a woman who had been on the executive team until she was hired away by another company. She had always been the "voice of the customer" and had communicated that the key customer wasn't happy. Somewhat embarrassed, Robert confessed that the rest of the executive team had discounted her input. "Now I see the different perspective and value she brought to our organization," he said and then concluded, "I think we need some balance on the leadership team."

In my leadership development and executive coaching practice, I see many talented executives and profitable organizations that have achieved measurable success and yet suddenly find themselves falling behind the market and the competition. Consistently, I find that the primary reason for this shift is that these leaders and organizations continue to rely on the same leadership approach that garnered them success in the past. And why shouldn't they? If it's not broken, don't fix it, right? While current leadership models aren't necessarily "broken," the reality is that they can't and won't drive success in today's business environment. In other words, what got you where you are isn't going to get you where you want to go in the future. The world is a very different place than it was just 10 short years ago. You simply can't run a successful company in today's complex global marketplace the same way you did in the past. The truth is that we can no longer use the same thought and decision-making processes and expect to be successful . . . *twentieth-century leadership models won't work for twenty-first-century organizations and twenty-first-century problems.* We need a different leadership model—a shift to a new model of leadership that gives organizations a better chance of not just surviving, but thriving, both now and in the years to come.

Successful organizations of the future will be led by *fully engaged, balanced teams of men and women working together synergistically to produce extraordinary results.* I call this Integrated Leadership. Leaders who create high-performing organizations and get lasting results are those who value and leverage the broad spectrum of gender intelligence—an intentional balance that enables an organization to deal with the complexities in today's marketplace. *A balanced, Integrated Leadership team is the new competitive advantage.*

So what happened to Robert and his organization? Through the course of our conversation, he came to understand that he had been operating with only half of his potential leadership capacity. He also realized that if his organization was going to continue to succeed in the future, he would need a broader range of leadership traits, thinking, and perspectives in order to respond to market dynamics, challenges, and opportunities.

In the following months, Robert worked to shift his leadership team. He brought on new leaders who possessed a diversity of perspectives, styles, and traits and represented both left- and right-brain thinking. With a balanced, Integrated Leadership team in place, over time his organization earned back customers it had lost, and it regained market share.

A New Approach to Leadership

The idea of a new leadership model is not only interesting; it is now essential for most organizations to be successful in our ever-changing and always challenging global business environment. I've interviewed more than 50 successful top executives on this topic and discovered that I'm not the only one who recognizes the urgency for a new approach to leadership. Many business leaders already sense that the leadership style that worked for them in the past is less effective in the context of today's realities. Gary Stuggins, executive vice president of the World Bank, shared with me that there is an underlying force causing organizations and leaders to rethink how they plan, make decisions, engage employees, and interact with clients. This new way of thinking and operating is reshaping leadership in organizations.

Dottie Brienza, chief diversity officer and head of Executive Talent at Merck (former senior vice president of Global Talent Management for Hilton International), shared a similar perspective:

> The level of complexity that organizations are dealing with, as well as the level of ambiguity and the challenges of our global focus, has increased significantly. If you think back about 20 years ago and consider typical Fortune 50–100 leaders, their job was probably very centric to the country in which they were operating. Maybe they were just starting to venture out in other parts of the globe. Or if they were already established in other parts of the world, the company was structured such that the local management in those areas was only worried about things that were happening in that part of the world. Now our leaders need to think about all the events happening around the world to determine and address their impact on all phases of their business operation. To do this, they have to integrate a variety of information sources into a more holistic perspective to determine appropriate courses of action—organizationally and interpersonally. This requires strong analytical skills along with a higher level of emotional intelligence than they have ever needed before.
>
> Our customers, like our planet, are diverse, with different likes and needs. If we only have one type of executive—whether that be all women, all male, all whatever—when we're dealing with human beings and relationships, we will be limited—only recognizing that narrow slice of the world—and we'll miss all kinds of opportunities, even conversations that are ultimately crucial to our success. And

as a result, we will miss a critical chance for the continuous learning that will keep us at the top of our industry today and give us that competitive advantage we need to remain there in the future. That's why I believe we need what you are calling "Integrated Leadership."

Gary and Dottie are not the only business leaders who are recognizing this requirement. Every day, we are experiencing dramatic shifts in our environment due to the increased complexity across our globe. Recent events have shown us how intricately linked the world is. From a natural resource perspective to a human perspective to a workplace perspective to a sociogeological perspective, these elements are all connected. The changing times in our world and work environments have created this need for a new way of thinking and leading. Without the unique perspectives and styles of both men and women, it will be very difficult for organizations to achieve success in the future. Melanie Healey, a senior executive at Procter & Gamble, agrees: "It's having this combination of very different perspectives that creates our next Wow! solution—the ideas that no one has ever thought before."

I had the opportunity to speak with Ted Hoff, who is the human resources vice president of Global Sales and Sales Incentives at IBM. I asked Ted his view on whether organizations have a greater competitive advantage with a more balanced leadership team in senior roles. Ted responded, "Absolutely! At a personal level, you need strengths in all aspects of both creative and analytical thinking or you have to overcome the shortfall by surrounding yourself with people that complement you, based on whatever your weaknesses are."

Ted said that it's important in today's economy to know how to identify and work with people who can expand your abilities. "We all have to be able to see new creative opportunities, set new directions, and inspire people to create innovative breakthroughs. We also have to manage the complexities of business and ensure that results are achieved on time and within a budget. We need the ability to do all of the above—so leadership teams that have strengths in both dimensions of human intelligence unquestionably have a competitive advantage."

Ted also shared with me that IBM has always looked at what distinguishes outstanding performance and exemplary leadership. To accomplish both, IBM established leadership competencies based on the behaviors that the company believes will make a difference in both personal and organizational performance. Ted told me, "When you look at these competencies, they are balanced. There's no question that some of them are on the creative/expansive side and some of them are on the analytical/execution side. This balance is what enables IBM to sustain great leadership teams that ensure we meet, and often exceed, our business goals."

What Melanie and Ted are pointing out for us is that the world we're living in today actually demands that organizations have a balanced, integrated approach to leadership. We don't have the luxury of not tapping into our full capacity as a leadership team. It will take a unified and integrated group of leaders who can leverage one another's unique strengths and integrate both the practical and the creative insights of different perspectives to be successful in our ever more complex and connected world.

The Business Case for Integrated Leadership

Now is the time to foster an Integrated Leadership culture—one that values, leverages, and blends the differences and attributes of both women and men. This need for a new approach to leadership dovetails with women's increasing presence and prominence. Women are becoming an important powerhouse in the business world. Consider the following:

- Women make over 80 percent of all consumer purchases.
- Women make up more than 50 percent of the U.S. workforce. By 2010, the number of women in the U.S. labor

force had increased by almost 10 million, a growth rate almost one-third higher than that of men.

- Women are graduating at twice the rate of men across all disciplines at the graduate and undergraduate levels.
- Women own more than 50 percent of nearly half the 10.6 million privately held companies in the United States. Between 1997 and 2004, the estimated growth rate in the number of women-owned businesses was nearly twice the rate of all firms.

So if you didn't think that women and women-owned firms are helping to power the economy, these statistics might begin to change your mind. Wherever you turn, women are influencing purchasing decisions, starting innovative businesses, and serving as major suppliers and clients. Savvy companies realize that value propositions that cater to women and to women-owned businesses are crucial, as women are a major consumer group and a major employer in the U.S. labor market.

Equally important is the overwhelming evidence supporting the importance and value of women in senior leadership. Multiple studies have proved that *organizations with more women in senior executive and board roles are more profitable, better adept at attracting and retaining top talent, and better able to grow and maintain their competitive advantage*:

- A McKinsey & Company report showed that companies with a higher proportion of women in top management positions have better financial performance. Specifically, companies with the most gender-diverse management teams had a 48 percent higher EBIT (earnings before interest and taxes), 10 percent higher ROE (return on equity), and a 1.7 times greater stock growth when compared with their industry averages.[1]

- According to a study published several years ago in *Harvard Business Review*, gender-diverse companies are 69 percent more profitable than other companies.
- Catalyst, a U.S. nonprofit research organization, found a 26 percent difference in return on invested capital between the top-quartile companies (which had 19–44 percent women board members) and bottom-quartile companies (which had no women board members).
- As reported by *USA Today*, the stocks of the 13 Fortune 500 companies that had a woman at the helm for all of 2009 were up an average 50 percent, significantly outperforming the S&P 500 (companies dominated by male chief executives), which was up only 25 percent.

As women are being recognized as an instrumental component of the leadership equation, research continues to validate that women leaders are just as capable as their male counterparts. In their blog *Are Women Better Leaders Than Men?*, noted authors Jack Zenger and Joseph Folkman (*The Inspiring Leader: Unlocking the Secrets of How Extraordinary Leaders Motivate*, McGraw-Hill, New York, 2009) revealed their latest research. In a survey of 7,280 leaders based on 360 evaluations, leaders were rated on 16 leadership competencies. They report:

At every [leadership] level, more women were rated by their peers, their bosses, their direct reports and their other associates as better overall leaders than their male counterparts—and the higher the level, the wider that gap grows.

At all levels, women are rated higher in 12 of the 16 competencies that go into outstanding leadership. And two of the traits where women outscored men to the highest degree—taking initiative and driving for results—have long been thought of as particularly male strengths. Men outscored women significantly on only one management competence in this survey—the ability to develop a strategic perspective. Why are women viewed as less strategic? Top leaders always score significantly higher in this competency; since more top leaders are men, men still score higher here in the aggregate. But when we measure only men and women in top management on strategic perspective, their relative scores are the same.[2]

There is also an increasing body of interesting research about how teams are more effective when women are involved. A *Harvard Business Review* article titled "What Makes a Team Smarter? More Women" indicates that having a balance of both men and women will create what many refer to as "cognitive diversity" for the group, and this factor alone has been proved to yield greater results.

Does this mean that women are smarter? Of course not! The specific study that this article cites indicates that there's little correlation between a group's collective intelligence and the IQs of its individual members. It's the social sensitivity that makes a team smarter. In fact, the researchers gave subjects (ages 18 to 60) standard intelligence tests and assigned them randomly to teams. Each team was asked to complete several tasks and was given intelligence scores based on performance. Though some teams had members with higher IQs, this did not help them to better solve important business issues.

What did make a significant difference was the element of social sensitivity, which many women tend to have a greater capacity for than do many men. What do women do that relates to this unique attribute? Well, for one thing, it seems that women tend to possess the natural skills for listening to each other. They also share constructive criticism more readily. They have open minds. They're not autocratic. All these characteristics directly relate to social sensitivity.

I want to note here that what is really important is to have people on your leadership team who are high in social sensitivity, whether they are men or women. Bringing greater social sensitivity into your team doesn't necessarily mean it has to be provided by women, but research shows that your chance of getting this type of thinking and behavior is greater if you're working with both men and women rather than just men. And as the *HBR* article indicates, if a group includes more women, its collective intelligence, based on the condition of social sensitivity, rises.

The skills and abilities that tend to come more naturally for women are becoming more pertinent, and some would even say "crucial," in the new business environment. Women's leadership strengths include creativity, patience, perseverance, intuition, empathy, social and relationship intelligence, a holistic view of the world, a keen sense of observation, the ability to see connections among people and situations, and a predisposition toward collaboration and inclusion.

Throughout the history of our society and culture, these strengths kept women out of higher levels of leadership. However, we are now seeing our world shift in a way that these very qualities, which women strongly possess, are needed in our organizations in order to create a better tomorrow.

An Integrated Approach to Integrated Leadership

Building an Integrated Leadership team requires a holistic, integrated, sustainable approach. It's not about "fixing" women, by, say, sending them to a leadership development program, nor is it about achieving diversity quotas. And this change is not just the responsibility of HR, although HR will certainly play a key role. Instead, Integrated Leadership requires everyone's involvement—women's, men's, and their organizations' involvement too:

- Women have leadership qualities that are both valuable and needed, and they must start showing up as the true leaders they are.

- Men need to realize the valuable role they play and be not only a part of the conversation but provide their leadership attributes and experiences with the women leaders in their organizations in creating balanced, integrated teams.
- Organizations must become more aware of and savvy about gender intelligence and its value. After they do this, they can then work to create a culture that leverages the best of both male and female leaders.

Integrated Leadership is about so much more than advancing women to the senior and executive ranks. It is about a new way of leading organizations, a new way of doing business. The rest of this book will examine how Integrated Leadership yields better business results and then go beyond theory to provide a detailed plan for implementing this new model.

Chapter Summary

- Current leadership models can't drive success in today's business environment because twentieth-century leadership models won't work for twenty-first-century organizations and twenty-first-century problems.
- Successful organizations of the future will be led by fully engaged, balanced teams of men *and women* working together synergistically to produce extraordinary results.
- Integrated Leadership—an approach that values, leverages, and blends the differences and attributes of both women and men—is the new competitive advantage.
- The business case for Integrated Leadership includes the following points:
  - Women are becoming an important powerhouse in the business world.

- ∘ Companies with the most gender-diverse management teams tend to consistently perform better and be more profitable than other companies.
- ∘ Studies prove that women leaders are just as capable as their male counterparts.
- ∘ The skills and abilities that tend to come more naturally for women are crucial in the new business environment.
- Building an Integrated Leadership team requires a holistic approach that includes women, men, and their organizations.

Notes

1. McKinsey & Company, "Women Matter: Gender Diversity, a Corporate Performance Driver," 2007.
2. http://blogs.hbr.org/cs/2012/03/a_study_in_leadership_women_do .html, Thursday, March 15, 2012.

Chapter 2

The Brain Science Behind the Integrated Leadership Model

WHEN WOMEN WORK side by side as equals with men, broader perspectives are heard, a wider range of skills is available, and more innovative thinking occurs. This, in turn, results in a more productive and invigorated work environment. The bottom line is this: a better balance of men and women in senior leadership roles drives higher profits and gives organizations a sustainable competitive advantage.

But why is this true? Why do women make a difference? Well, maybe it's because . . . they are different from men! Is there anyone left on this planet who doesn't know that men and women are different? Doubtful! Men and women think and act differently, and hence they get different results. But *why* do women think differently from men? It's really pretty simple. It ultimately involves the brain.

Over the last several decades, advanced brain research has taught us a tremendous amount about how the human brain functions. Basically the human brain is divided into two hemispheres: left and right. We use both sides of our brains for the most simple and the most challenging tasks, but most people tend to be dominant on one side. Left-brain dominance is often described as analytical, sequential, logical, and detailed. Right-brain dominance is described as creative, nonlinear, intuitive, and holistic.

Until the early 1990s, it was thought that all brains were the same. However in the late 1980s, the MRI (magnetic resonance imaging) was invented, and MRI scans dramatically changed the thinking around male and female brains. This new technology was able to demonstrate, repeatedly, that there are specific ways the male and female brain are inherently different. In fact, neurobiologists have been able to track more than a hundred biological differences between the male and female brain.

Later, in 1995, a team at Yale determined that men tend to primarily use the left side of the brain and women tend to use both the left and right sides. Since a man's brain functions are dominant in the left hemisphere, he is more likely to rely on logic-based thinking and fact-based approaches and have a preference for a more detailed orientation. Since women switch back and forth, between left and right hemispheres, they are more likely to have a broader, big-picture orientation, to have stronger emotions and feelings, and to use their intuition a great deal. Researchers also found that women are able to pick up on more sensory cues (such as facial cues) than men, which helps them to better understand what others are thinking and feeling.

Different Brains Mean Different Behaviors

Years of research and studies indicate that the structures of the male and female brain are different, which determines how the two genders think, what they value, and how they communicate. Studies indicate that men and women produce the same intellectual performance but that their brains do it differently. Most people react to these unique differences rather than taking the time to understand the root cause of them, such as the wiring of our brains. Let me explain what I mean when I say "differences."

- **Communication.** Women speak up to 6,000 to 8,000 words per day and use 8,000 to 10,000 gestures and body language signals a day. On the other hand, men speak only 2,000 to 4,000 words a day and use between 2,000 and 3,000 gestures and body language signals a day.

- **Emotions.** Women's brains tend to have more emotional activity that takes place in the middle of the brain (the limbic system), and men have more rational activity that takes place in the top of the brain (the cerebral cortex).

- **Compartmentalizing versus multitasking.** Men tend to compartmentalize more brain activity and focus on one task, whereas women more naturally multitask.

- **Attention to details.** Women tend to take in more information through their five senses than men do and store more of that information in the brain for other uses. Therefore, they have more interest in and pay more attention to details.

- **Stress.** Men tend to deal with stress much more easily than women, as it's harder for women to shut down their autostress response.

- **Logic versus language.** Men tend to have better logic skills than women, and women tend to have better language skills than men.

Let's look at one of these factors a little bit closer. In my prior book, *It's Not a Glass Ceiling, It's a Sticky Floor*, I explained that the average person spends 80 percent of his or her time communicating each day. However, over 60 percent of that communication is misconstrued, sends people in the wrong direction, or causes relationship problems. Based on the wiring of our brain, one of the biggest differences between males and females is the way we communicate. Here are a few differences that you may recognize:

Communication Dynamic	Men	Women
Conversation	Tend to talk to exchange information	Tend to talk to express their thoughts and feelings
Listening	Equate listening with getting the results they desire—it is a means to an end	Think of listening as simply giving others an opportunity to share their thoughts and feelings
Inquiry	Asking what another person thinks means the questioner has no additional thoughts or doesn't have a strong conviction	Asking what another person thinks is a way of opening the discussion, engaging the other person, and expanding potential ideas
Apology	See apologies as showing weakness, lacking confidence, or admitting fault	See apologies as restoring balance and being polite

These examples illustrate how men and women communicate differently based on what thousands of neurologists, psychologists, and linguists say about our brain differences. I would add here that equally as important in understanding these differences is recognizing that boys and girls are socialized differently while growing up, which also reinforces many of these differences. I'll talk more about this later in the book because the implications of these communication differences are pretty significant on leadership teams. For example, I hear over and over again from women that they speak up at a meeting but men don't seem to be listening. As you can now imagine, there might be several things going on here!

How Gender-Based Brain Differences Play Out in Leadership

While the applications of brain research are many, perhaps none is more fascinating than how brain research and human intelligence affect leadership, especially as it relates to male and female leaders. Millions of dollars have been invested in research around the gender brain functions that directly impact essential leadership skills such as communication, analytical and innovative thinking, and decision making, just to name a few.

The differences between men's and women's brains explain the considerable differences in how they operate in the workplace—how they lead, communicate, act, react, problem-solve, make decisions, and work together. Different brains drive different behaviors, which lead to different outcomes. Men tend to be more competitive, evidence based, results oriented, and present focused. Women, on the other hand, tend to be more collaborative, intuitive, empathetic, and future focused. Certainly, both men and women can and do possess the traits of both genders, but because of their brain structure, each gender is geared toward natural tendencies.

As I was reviewing research for this book, I was interested in how the brain impacts men and women in terms of the traits we associate with strong leaders. The following information about the differences between men and women summarizes brain research, as well as my own observations and experiences working closely with business leaders for the past 20 years. See if any of this information surprises you. More likely, it will just validate what you already know!

Leadership Factor	Men	Women
Leadership Style	Tend to think about who's in charge and view an organization in terms of hierarchy and structure. Are more direct in nature.	Tend to be more participatory and collaborative. They have the ability to demonstrate a more "coachlike" leadership style.
Problem Solving	Tend to move more quickly to the ultimate goal and spend less time considering the individual pieces of the problem	Able to see all the different pieces of a problem and how they interconnect as a part of the whole
Decision Making	Tend to be more deductive and make decisions based on facts, data, and logic. They are more comfortable dealing with ambiguity.	Tend to be more inductive and able to make decisions based on gut or intuition. They tend to listen and connect the different points of view when making decisions.

(continued)

Leadership Factor	Men	Women
Relationships	Tend to be more transactional in their interactions. Once the transaction is completed, they get back to the task at hand rather than remaining with the person for social reasons.	Tend to be more interactive and to value the emotional aspects of relationships. They also tend to seek more interpersonal interactions on a day-to-day basis.
Self-Promotion	Tend to be comfortable defining themselves by their strengths and accomplishments. This can be defined as "self-promotion," which is generally more natural for men.	Tend not to self-promote themselves but rather talk about the strengths and accomplishments of their team or colleagues
Observation	Often listen without as much facial attentiveness as women exhibit. Women tend to feel not heard by men who listen with a blank face.	Tend to be good at reading social cues such as facial expressions and can sometimes read more into them than may be true
Managing Stress	Tend to manage stress or solve more personal problems by dealing with it alone versus talking about it with other people	Tend to manage stress by reaching out to others to talk about what they are dealing with

There are many disconnects between men and women on leadership teams that are based on assumptions and subsequent judgments we make about each other. Understanding a little about the brain and these specific brain differences helps us to both appreciate the opposite sex and tolerate our gender differences in light of the payback we get for leveraging each other's strengths. If we recognized and appreciated our differences, we could build a bridge that would allow us to leverage the best of each other. Imagine, if we did this, how we could have more productive meetings, more effective problem solving, better business decisions, and, perhaps best of all, a greater facility for embracing and leading change in our organizations.

Whole Brain® Thinking

I don't want to bore you with pages of scientific brain research, but I do want to mention the work of Ned Herrmann, author of *The Whole Brain® Business Book* (McGraw-Hill, New York, 1996), who, while working at General Electric, pioneered the study of the brain and its impact in business. Herrmann took the concept of left- and right-brain dominance one step further. Through his research he developed a powerful metaphor and model of the brain showing four specialized thinking clusters, or quadrants, that control the way we learn, view the world, interpret and process information, and interact with others. These four areas correlate to specific thinking preferences: (A) analytical and logical, (B) organized and task oriented, (C) intuitive and relationship oriented (emotional intelligence), and (D) creative and big-picture oriented.

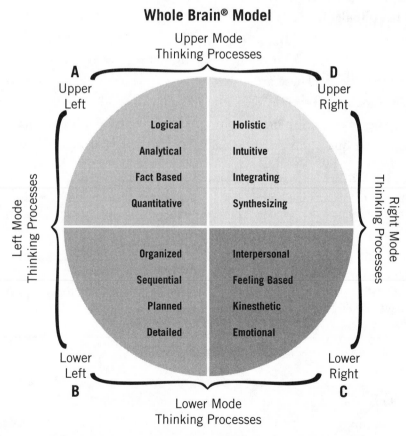

Whole Brain® Model

Upper Mode
Thinking Processes

Source: Herrmann International, Whole Brain® Model. The Whole Brain® Model graphic and 4-color 4-quadrant graphic are trademarks of Herrmann Global, LLC © 2012, www.HerrmannInternational.com.

The different quadrants of the Whole Brain® Model explain why people have significantly different ways they perceive and assimilate information, problem-solve, make decisions, communicate, and behave. Knowing and appreciating these different thinking styles can significantly influence the way you lead individuals and teams, as well as how you harness the unique yet different human intelligences across your organization and with your customers.

You may already have a good idea about the dominant aspects of your brain. Herrmann's research measuring thinking preferences with the HBDI® (Herrmann Brain Dominance Instrument) assessment has proven that we have access to all four quadrants, and only 3 percent of the population equally prefers all four. The data show that CEOs frequently fall into this group. Most of us have one, two, or three that we prefer most. Which of these quadrants resonate with you more than the others? These areas tend to link to your thinking-style preferences, which in turn lead to a set of behaviors and often those competencies you develop most easily. Here is another simple explanation of the four quadrants and how each translates to particular behaviors:

A Quadrant: Financial, bottom line, technology based	**D Quadrant:** Clear vision, effective strategy, breakthrough ideas and products, and success at a global level
B Quadrant: On-time completion, tactical excellence, and zero defect quality	**C Quadrant:** Customer-, employee-, community-satisfaction, moral issues, and effective teams and communication

Source: Herrmann International, Whole Brain® Model

One of the key principles of Herrmann's Whole Brain® Thinking methodology concept is that when we utilize all four quadrants of the brain, we are more efficient and productive and perform better.

In fact, most successful CEOs in today's marketplace can use their entire brain. And just as individuals achieve better results when they use all parts of their brain, so too do organizations perform better and achieve better results when they utilize and leverage the characteristics of the four quadrants of the brain.

Apple founder and longtime leader Steve Jobs inherently understood the value of Whole Brain® Thinking long before anyone was talking about it. In his article "The Real Leadership Lessons of Steve Jobs," Walter Isaacson stated: "He connected the humanities to the sciences, creativity to technology, arts to engineering. There were greater technologists (Wozniak, Gates), and certainly better designers and artists. But no one else in our era could better firewire together poetry and processors in a way that jolted innovation. And he did it with an intuitive feel for business strategy. At almost every product launch over the past decade, Jobs ended with a slide that showed a sign at the intersection of Liberal Arts and Technology Streets."[1]

Rich DeSerio, manager of IBM's Global Design Team for Leadership Development, told me that Whole Brain® Thinking is an approach that IBM has used successfully in its global leadership development programs. Rich said, "IBM's globally integrated workforce gives it a competitive advantage in serving clients." He continued, "To be truly global requires that all IBMers be culturally adaptable in all its forms. This extends beyond just understanding our cultural diversity to using this diversity to extend our competitive advantage. Whole Brain® Thinking allows us to understand, appreciate, and, most important, leverage the diversity of thought that naturally exists in our company. Whole Brain® Thinking also shows us that we all learn differently, that we all have access to different thinking preferences, and that we need to flex our thinking when the situation demands it. With a common understanding of thinking preferences and the benefits of Whole Brain® Thinking, people see the necessity and utility of diverse thought. At that point, we can begin fully leveraging the individual."[2]

If you're familiar with the organizational "scorecard," you'll notice that it actually illustrates the importance of Whole Brain® Thinking by recognizing that it takes a diverse and integrated set of behaviors to focus and successfully drive performance. *Integrated Leadership is the way to achieve Whole Brain® Thinking at an organizational level.* All four quadrants are important, and every strong leadership team needs to be composed of individuals who, together, represent this Whole Brain® Thinking capability. It's the *integration* of different ways of thinking that creates a more natural equilibrium—where business problems get solved, where the impossible becomes possible, and where the ultimate solution benefits the greater good.

Chapter Summary

- Integrated Leadership is supported by brain-based research.
- Men and women think and act differently because their brains are physiologically different.
- The differences between men's and women's brains explain the considerable differences in how they think, what they value, and how they operate in the workplace, including how they lead, communicate, act, react, problem-solve, make decisions, and work together.
- Generally speaking, men tend to be more competitive, evidence based, results oriented, and present focused. Women tend to be more collaborative, intuitive, empathetic, and future focused.
- The principle of Whole Brain® Thinking tells us that when we utilize all four of the brain's quadrants, we are more efficient and productive and perform better. Likewise, organizations perform better and achieve better results when they utilize and leverage the characteristics of the four

quadrants of the Whole Brain® approaches they each have available to them.

- Integrated Leadership achieves Whole Brain® Thinking at an organizational level.

Notes

1. Walter Isaacson, "The Real Leadership Lessons of Steve Jobs," *Harvard Business Review*, April 2012.
2. Ann Herrmann-Nehdi, "Whole Brain® Thinking: Ignore It at Your Peril." *American Society for Training & Development, T&D Magazine*, May 2010.

Chapter 3

The Benefits
of Integrated Leadership

IF WE OVERLAY the concept of Whole Brain® Thinking with the brain differences between men and women, we discover the scientific evidence behind the Integrated Leadership Model, which embraces and leverages the strengths of both men and women leaders. When organizations adopt this Integrated Leadership approach, there is a significant, positive effect. I call this the *Integration Quotient*:

Male Traits + Female Traits = Better Business Outcomes

For example, attaining great customer loyalty requires us to research trends around customer buying patterns, analyze market data, calculate costs, and determine competitive pricing—all while also building meaningful relationships and using every ounce of our emotional intelligence to build trust with clients and to consistently demonstrate the mutual benefits of doing business together. Here are just a few examples of how the Integration Quotient can produce better results for leadership teams:

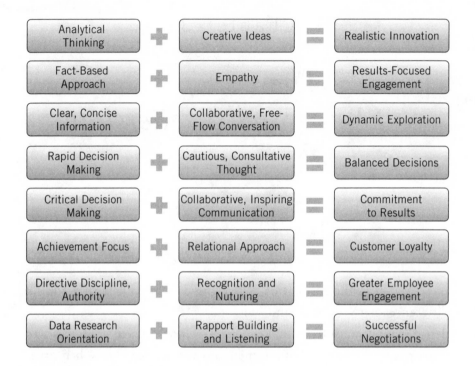

As I mentioned in the last chapter, IBM has recognized the bene-fits of an Integrated Leadership approach for many years and has created a culture in many parts of the organization where men and women recognize each other's strengths and leverage them in everyday activities. Through thoughtful and targeted training, this concept has become a reality. Let me give you an example.

Rich DeSerio shared with me how his team of nine people around the world work together: "My team and I are fairly balanced. Even with a small group of nine, I have people who are way out on the cre-ativity side, and then I have others who can solve any problem with math. Getting those people together to work on a program design produces the opportunity for integration. Even in my small team, I see the benefit of having a Whole Brain® team. Perfect example, we might be scratching our heads thinking about something and saying we have to come up with something different and then we'll say, 'Why don't we ask Deb?' Deb is usually good with a blank sheet of paper. It doesn't matter what we're trying to do; she'll usually bounce out a couple of good ideas. Then, we'll say, 'OK, well now we have to get Paul in the loop to provide the market research, run a detailed budget, and create a financial model.' And it's all done in a very open and honest way. With this integrated approach, we have been able to accomplish state-of-the-art leadership programs and sustainable learning solutions for IBMers."

Like Rich and his team, most of us leading organizations need to find a way to combine creative and innovative thinking with the capacity to successfully implement those ideas. Rich said, "At IBM, we need the kind of rapid innovation that separates great organizations from ordinary ones. We know what happens to the ordinary ones. They disappear."

Integrated Leadership Benefits All

What many business leaders don't realize is that if we all had a deeper awareness of the differences between men and women that help drive Integrated Leadership, we would reap the benefits from these different perspectives at the organizational, team, and individual levels. Here are just a few examples of how this knowledge can benefit organizations and teams:

- **Organizational change efforts.** Change in organizations is a constant reality. Yet leaders continue to struggle when leading people through continued and complex change. Taking a balanced approach by providing the facts (and not sugarcoating the realities pertaining to the impact of the change) while balancing that information with empathy with peoples' sense of loss, inherent fears, and multifaceted frustration is essential for helping them to accept or support the change and do what is necessary to successfully implement the change.

- **Negotiations.** Organizations negotiate on a regular basis. Being aware of the different thinking styles of negotiators, along with having a balanced leadership approach in both the planning and execution of the negotiation experience, results in a fact-based and research orientation along with relational energy, emotional interpretation, and active listening, which are all critical for producing win-win agreements.

- **Team effectiveness.** For a team to achieve its potential and become high performing, it's important that the members understand the thinking-style preferences of their colleagues so they can more effectively work together to complement one another and seek what's "missing" from those who are outside the team.

And if you need more reasons to embrace and act on an integrated approach, here are a few for individuals:

- **Career development.** Understanding our natural tendencies, unique strengths, and basic assumptions helps us understand why we are better at some things than others, why we are motivated to get involved in certain tasks and tend to tune out other activities, and why we are recognized for certain kinds of contributions rather than others. People often find that knowing this information helps them in creating their career goals and choosing development activities in a way that ensures a more synergistic alignment with their natural traits and interests. By understanding our brains' dominant traits, we are more confident in using our strengths, more accepting of our weaknesses, and more tolerant of the differences of others.

- **Influence, persuasion, and communication.** Having a better understanding of different thinking styles can help us be more effective influencing and persuading others. For example, while one person will prefer lots of data and facts in order to buy into an idea, another person will simply want to be briefed on the big picture. Understanding these differences in ourselves and learning how to recognize them in others enables us to tailor our influence approach accordingly.
- **Career and work-life balance.** Many people have made career decisions based on factors such as pay, perks, or location. Yet research suggests that the most effective people succeed because they are in jobs that they are suited to and enjoy. By understanding our neurological dominance profile, we are better able to match our career choices to our personal profile, thereby reducing our stress and improving our performance.

You and Integrated Leadership

SHAMBAUGH's Leadership Programs and Coaching Practice help business leaders identify their own brain-related leadership traits and leadership and communication styles, as well as those of their team members, to ensure that they have the right balance for the best possible results. If you lead an organization and are interested in attaining Integrated Leadership, ask yourself the following questions:

- *How balanced is my leadership team? What is the proportion of men to women?*
- *How much do I know about the inherent differences between the male and female brain and the way these differences play out in terms of different styles and behaviors? What else do I want to learn?*

- *Does my team composition provide a wide enough spectrum of thinking styles, traits, dispositions, strengths, and behaviors to ensure we are achieving integrated outcomes? What do we have, and what is missing?*
- *Do the members of my team understand the different thinking styles among themselves and the importance of capitalizing on those differences to attain maximum results and ultimate success? How can I help them to become more aware and take appropriate action based on this?*
- *What can I do to attain greater balance and take advantage of the Integrated Leadership Model to ensure that I maximize the potential of all my team members?*

Chapter Summary

- The benefits of Integrated Leadership can be represented by the Integration Quotient: Male Traits + Female Traits = Better Business Outcomes.
- Integrated Leadership benefits the organization as well as teams and individuals.
- Better balanced leadership leads to better business results.

Chapter 4

Where Are the Women?

MY HOPE IS THAT I've made the business case that Integrated Leadership—men and women working synergistically together on leadership teams—is what will separate those organizations that will grow and thrive from those that will be left behind. My hope is also that you now see that *better balanced leadership leads to better business results.* But therein lies the challenge!

After all these years, organizations are still not balanced at the senior and executive leadership levels. In their 2011 research, noted earlier, Jack Zenger and Joseph Folkman found: "The majority of leaders (64 percent) are still men. And the higher the level, the more men there are . . . 78 percent of top managers were men, 67 percent at the next level down (that is, senior executives reporting directly to the top managers), 60 percent at the manager level below that."

With all the transformation going on in organizations over the past few years, it amazes me that we still only have a handful of female executives and CEOs in the Fortune 500 companies. The number of women in executive suites and on boards of U.S. companies is no higher today than it was a decade ago and in some cases is actually lower. Based on a recent Catalyst report, 15.4 percent of women hold corporate officer positions, 15.4 percent hold corporate board seats,

6.7 percent of women are top wage earners, and 2.4 percent of women are Fortune 500 CEOs.

I spoke with Linda Tarr-Whelan, who is a speaker and an author on women's leadership issues and who served on the UN Commission on the Status of Women in the Clinton administration. Under President Jimmy Carter, she was a White House deputy assistant focusing on women's concerns, and in that role she discussed her concept of the 30 percent solution. Linda shared with me that when women represent just 30 percent of the senior leadership team or board of an organization, real change starts to happen, and the organization begins to see a positive shift in terms of organizational performance, market share, and enhanced competitive advantage. Having an additional 30 percent of women's thinking and leadership style creates a different, yet important, balance that creates a better output. This does not mean that a woman's view is any better than a man's. What's important is having the diversity of views and perspectives to balance out the thinking, problem solving, and decision making. Sadly, we haven't yet reached this tipping point, and we are in fact far from it.

Our business environment and society have been talking about gender (and cultural) diversity for years now. And yet women are still grossly underrepresented in the senior leadership ranks. Despite the fact that 50 percent of the workforce is composed of women and women hold close to 50 percent of all managerial positions in the Fortune 500 companies, women make up only 14 percent of senior executive roles. Men still represent 80 percent of the executive suite and corporate boards and hold 87 percent of the line officer positions.

When I look at these statistics, what really concerns me is the lack of balance in our leadership thinking, decision making, and problem solving (not to mention the issue of not having enough women in senior roles to mentor other women and to encourage them to seek higher positions). What this means, in effect, is that organizations have been using only half their "brain"—or leadership capacity—because most senior leadership teams have been predominantly composed of men. Now some people will tell you that this approach has worked. My question is this: how successful would you be if you were only using half your brain? Not very!

The realities of today's business environment demand a balanced leadership approach, and yet most leadership teams today continue to look and act much like they did decades ago. So why do we still have a gap between what leadership teams *should* look like and what they *actually do look like*? Why aren't more women advancing to the senior leadership ranks?

What Is the Problem?

Over the past few years, I have spoken with hundreds of women who are both eager to learn and ready to take on greater leadership responsibility. They are bright, hardworking, successful managers and team leaders, and they possess the high-achievement characteristics that organizations look for in leaders. In fact, many organizations have invested significantly in these high-potential women and have developed a robust leadership pipeline of competent women.

However, it seems that when women get to the brink of advancing to more senior levels, they either don't apply for the opportunity, get passed over, or are given the responsibility but not the title. Something is happening with women in the leadership pipeline when they get to the point of advancing to the senior level. But what is going on exactly?

First, our society is still hardwired with the traditional biases and assumptions that put men and women in separate (and different) "boxes," as opposed to one common box of potential leadership greatness. This mindset limits the possibilities for achieving a balanced leadership model that values and blends the unique attributes of both men and women. But men are beginning to see things differently. Maybe this is because as times are changing, their own daughters are entering the management ranks. Or perhaps they are recognizing that they must tap into the talent pool of women for potential successors. Whatever the case, men are beginning to change their minds. This is a process and slow to change, but there is a trend that we will continue to see with men.

The second part of the problem is that women have their own "Sticky Floors" when it comes to reaching higher levels of leadership. These Sticky Floors are the self-limiting beliefs, assumptions, and behaviors that hold women back from achieving their key goals and career objectives. In my first book, I defined and socialized the Sticky Floors concept for women who are in midrange management positions. It makes sense to now explore the things that hold women back from more senior positions. I call these "Sticky Floors 2.0," and they involve a completely different set of challenges, opportunities, and dynamics from the Sticky Floors I addressed in my first book. In this book, I want to encourage women to take more control of their destiny and declare their value and rightful position on senior leadership teams.

But there are at least two additional factors that keep women out of senior leadership roles, and they do *not* directly relate to women. These factors point to the fact that the dearth of women in senior leadership is not just a women's problem—it's everyone's problem.

Truth be told, men play a significant role in this situation. Quite frankly, how could they not? The vast majority of senior and executive leaders are men. Given their sheer numbers, one must logically conclude that men have some kind of impact or influence on the lack of women in leadership—but not in the way that you might think. Generally speaking, I don't subscribe to the idea that men intentionally keep women down or have stacked the system against them. Instead, I suggest that men are not aware of the significant role they play and therefore do not see themselves as a major part of the solution to this problem.

And finally, while most organizations have done a commendable job of providing leadership development and diversity training to fill the leadership pipeline with qualified candidates, organizations and their predominantly male leaders have not truly bought into the business case for actually advancing more women to the senior levels of leadership.

What Is the Solution?

We could sit back and wait for corporate cultures to embrace this critical change to Integrated Leadership, but studies predict that at the rate we are currently advancing women to the senior ranks, it will take 400 years for women to reach parity with men! For years I have heard the talk about embracing diversity and creating inclusive work environments and teams, because doing so would drive business results. But I don't see companies "walking the walk." It's time for organizations and their top leaders to move from conversation to action. Finding the right leadership balance does not just happen. Organizations and leaders have to see the value of it and be intentional in terms of creating a mindset around the culture of the business and the development and advancement of its leaders.

So how can we develop a more Integrated Leadership approach—one that encompasses the strengths of both men and women? The shift to Integrated Leadership will require the efforts of everyone. Ilene H. Lang, president and CEO of Catalyst, said, "The preponderance of men in leadership means their efforts are necessary to advance the change we need in the workplace to achieve Integrated Leadership. Research continues to show that well-managed diversity in an organization yields more innovation and is tied to enhanced financial performance—factors good for all employees."

Integrated Leadership is not only a women's issue—it applies to everyone. Consequently, everyone—men, women, and the organizations for which they work—must play a key role in the solution:

- *Women* must assume responsibility for their own career advancement. While a glass ceiling may still exist in some organizations, most women are stuck on a Sticky Floor of self-limiting assumptions, beliefs, and behaviors that prevent them from realizing their potential and moving to the next level of leadership. They must look within, acknowledge their leadership attributes, and then confidently take a seat at the table.
- *Men,* who represent over 80 percent of senior and executive leadership and corporate boards of directors, play a crucial role in helping women advance to higher-level leadership positions. These men are in the best position to advocate for women, and we need to tap into their insights, their goodwill, and their coaching and mentoring.
- *Organizations* must address the number of women who are dropping out of, or not signing up for, the senior leadership ranks. Many organizations have invested in and developed a robust leadership pipeline of competent women. Now they must take the next step and proactively seek ways to advance more women.

The rest of this book will focus on how the Integrated Leadership Model can be successfully implemented. It will offer specific strategies to take the idea from concept to reality. It will provide men with the strategies and tools necessary to create powerful synergies with women in order to build transformational, integrated senior leadership teams for their organizations. And it will provide women with specific strategies, tools, and techniques for raising their personal leadership quotient so they can rise to higher positions. To do this, men will be an important vehicle not only to help women see their potential but to help pull them up to the senior levels of leadership. To do this, women must look within themselves and determine what they are doing (or not doing) that is holding them back and then map out a plan to achieve what they define as success in their careers.

Chapter Summary

- Women are still grossly underrepresented in the senior leadership ranks relative to their numbers in the workforce and in managerial positions.
- Women are not advancing into the senior ranks because:
  - Our society is still hardwired with traditional biases and assumptions about men and women.
  - Women are stuck on their Sticky Floors—self-limiting beliefs, assumptions, and behaviors that hold them back from achieving their key goals and career objectives.
  - Organizations and their predominantly male leaders have not truly bought into the business case for balanced leadership.
- To build gender-diverse, Integrated Leadership teams, everyone must play a role in the solution:
  - Women must assume responsibility for their own career advancement.
  - Men, who represent the vast majority of senior and executive leadership, are in the best position to coach, mentor, and advocate for women.
  - Organizations must proactively seek ways to develop and advance more women into the senior ranks.

Part I Summary

In Part I, I have proposed that organizations strive to attain *Integrated Leadership*—men and women on leadership teams working together synergistically to achieve extraordinary results. This means that more women will need to assume some of these senior leadership positions if organizations and teams are to reap the potential benefits. My hope is that I have set out a convincing case for making this happen!

We have taken a simple look at the findings of brain research that indicate men and women are wired to think differently and that both ways of thinking—Whole Brain® Thinking—are essential for success in today's business environment. This concept of cognitive diversity is the foundation of what I call the Integrated Leadership Model, which harnesses the collective human intelligence available to us on Integrated Leadership teams. As leadership teams, I invite you to start leveraging the strengths of all team members. There's strength in each gender, just as there's strength in life experiences, age experiences, racial experiences, ethnicity, culture, and so many other aspects of life that make us who we are.

Successful organizations know how to intentionally leverage their greatest resource—people! The most progressive and savvy companies appreciate that consciously cultivating a broader mix of leaders will make them better at meeting consumer demands and positioning themselves in the marketplace. Many are viewing an Integrated Leadershp culture not as the *right* thing to do but as the *smart* thing to do. They know that as a result, they will be better able to take advantage of opportunities in a continuously evolving business world.

However, to get to where we need to be, it will call for all of us to look for the best thinking of all contributors. What I'm suggesting is the purest sense of integrating and blending all the different abilities of the leadership team into *one* powerful force. The rest of this book focuses on exactly how to do this.

Part II

Integrated Leadership: Men's Role

Chapter 5

Give Men a Chance!

Men Are Not the Problem . . .
They Are Part of the Solution

It's time for men to actively participate in the process of advancing more women to the leadership ranks and creating a balanced, integrated senior leadership team. Interestingly, men typically are not seen as playing a significant role in advancing women into leadership—that job has been left to the Human Resource or Organization Development department. There's no question that organizations have invested a lot of time and resources in diversity initiatives, as well as women's leadership and networking programs. Despite all these efforts, I believe that organizations have really missed the mark, primarily because they have not invited men to be cocreators of a better balance of leadership within teams and across the enterprise. Because men have been pushed to the sidelines, they have perhaps become apathetic about supporting women. Yet men are in the best position to mentor and sponsor women because they have spent the most time in the leadership ranks and hold the greatest knowledge and experience.

Jimmie Paschall, who is the executive vice president of Enterprise Diversity and Inclusion at Wells Fargo, shared with me, "Men need to be a part of what's being created and a part of the dialogue when it comes to diversity and development of women leaders. If we put men outside of the process, how can we expect them to be a part of the solution?"

This failure to engage men as a part of the solution might have unintentionally alienated a number of men who, in most cases, constitute the most powerful stakeholder group in large corporations. A male executive at J&J explained, "It's interesting . . . if I look back at my years as a manager in my prior company, we had a lot of diversity initiatives for women and yet they really didn't include men in any of those programs or conversations. This put some (particularly young) men on the defensive, and if they allowed it to, they could really become paranoid and feel intentionally left out. So, for me, what's most important in working toward a more balanced team of leaders (helping to advance women) is having men as an integral part of the equation."

To make a real difference today, men and women together need to change their mindset and realize that we aren't going to make sustainable progress if we only rely on women to change the status quo. As I have said for years, to see the change we are striving for, we *all* need to be part of the solution. In other words, both men and women need to work in partnership to break down old cultural barriers, address gender-related stereotypes, and essentially help each other realize their roles in closing the gender gap to achieve a better balance of leadership intelligence.

How Organizations Can Engage Men

As an organization, if you are looking at how to engage men in the effort of advancing women to senior positions, just bring them into the conversation! I know from experience that once invited, they engage willingly and powerfully!

Several years ago, SHAMBAUGH was hired to help an organization address its need to further develop and advance women in the leadership pipeline. The organization was also experiencing a significant turnover of top women in sales and had very few women moving into sales management. Recognizing that the leadership role in the company was demanding and stressful, it had invested in career development initiatives for women, including industry-specific education, professional competencies (such as time management), and personal development (such as work-life balance). And still the company was experiencing a higher attrition rate of talented women than was anticipated.

We conducted a series of interviews and focus groups to try to get at the heart of the matter. I remember so clearly the day that the SHAMBAUGH team and I presented to the organization's head of diversity and other senior-level staff. We walked through what we understood to be their goals in terms of developing, advancing, and retaining women leaders and then mapped out a plan that included a series of targeted sessions and focused coaching for women. They were fine with our ideas.

Then I shared that while they had traditionally focused on women helping women, it was important to bring men into the effort. Since most of the people in the room were men, it shouldn't have been a surprise that their reaction wasn't *why* but *how*! Since most of the women in the leadership pipeline had men as their managers, just about all the men in our audience had high-potential women working for them and were more than willing to become engaged in their success. But the problem was that they hadn't been asked and had no idea what they might do differently.

To make a very long story short, we implemented a structured program for women. And we also engaged men in the process. We brought men up to speed on the Sticky Floors and on effective coaching skills as well as on how to be a powerful sponsor and mentor. We invited them to roundtable discussions with women, where all the participants explored common challenges that women in business face and where the men could openly share their insights and advice. We also created mentoring pods, where the discussions could continue on a more personal level.

And the results were pretty impressive: 90 percent of the women who started the program completed it. As for the organization, it was able to retain several of its top female sales reps who were considering other job offers because they felt their careers weren't going anywhere; more women began applying for management positions because they were willing to take the risk knowing they had internal support and mentoring; and 25 percent of the women in the program were promoted into operational and P&L roles within less than a year after completing it.

Now, more than ever before, it's important for us to ask ourselves: *have women taken the time to help men understand how their roles can be pivotal in helping women to succeed in their careers and advance to greater levels of leadership?*

What Men Can Learn from Women

Men want to be part of successful organizations. The smart ones know that a balanced leadership team leads to better business outcomes. They recognize the value of having women on their executive teams from this business perspective as well as a leadership advantage.

Savvy men also know that they can benefit from a woman's insights and natural abilities and recognize what they can learn from women. SHAMBAUGH did a study in 2011 regarding what men thought were the five most beneficial things they learned from their female colleagues. Here they are.

1. How to Be a Better Listener

While listening has always been important in business, it has become imperative in today's world economy, where we don't have all the answers and it's almost impossible to predict the future. One of the keys to effective listening is being curious. In one of my interviews, I spoke with Robert Mattson, who works for a venture capital firm. Robert said, "Listening is one of the most important leadership traits for being successful in today's business environment since we don't have much margin for error. We win or lose by truly understanding and delivering what the customer is looking for."

Robert also shared that listening can be difficult for most men and that he learned the importance of it from a female mentor. He continued, "One of the things she taught me was how effective listening skills can be in helping you better understand how all the different pieces and events fit together. Asking the right questions, listening to both the content and the feelings of responses, and then questioning in greater depth is a critical leadership skill for all of us. And women are great role models for doing this."

2. How to Be Empathetic

Today's workforce is multigenerational, less trusting of leadership than in the recent past, and increasingly disengaged. These trends have created the need for a more empathetic approach to leadership in terms of daily interactions. And yet having empathy with others and helping people develop empathy are attributes that are still undervalued and missing in many organizations. Thankfully, the male executives I spoke with seemed to get it.

A study conducted by Hay Consulting indicated that the coaching style of leadership was one of the two most powerful styles (the other being visionary) and that women had a greater capacity than men to demonstrate this coaching style based on their emotional quotient (EQ).

A male executive told me, "I think women have a much greater awareness about themselves and can be open to making themselves vulnerable in a situation. The fact that women can be comfortable enough to do this is a gift because it allows them to show genuine empathy. And others sense this authenticity in daily interactions as well as in difficult coaching situations. For a man, it's much easier to get right to problem solving rather than taking the time to be empathetic."

I think he's right. This whole sense of self-awareness, which speaks to women's Whole Brain® Thinking, enables women to empathize with others more easily, which allows them to understand not only what is being said but what someone really means, so that they can acknowledge that person's concerns, fears, and deep-rooted values. This helps to build trusting and supportive relationships, which positively impacts employee satisfaction and job performance. Male executives have read enough about this very important cause-and-effect relationship that they value learning more about empathy from their female colleagues.

3. How to Foster Better Communication and Collaboration

Organizations and institutions are evolving from the hierarchical model to a more matrixed structure that directly impacts leadership roles, responsibilities, and styles. Many leaders today are finding that you can't use the traditional style of command and control to gain a lasting sense of commitment or to foster engagement. You need to communicate with people in a way that works for them. You also need to actively and meaningfully involve them in problem solving, decision making, and innovation activities. According to the body of brain research, these are skills (communication and collaboration) that many women naturally possess and inherently have a greater capacity to demonstrate as compared with men.

Let's look at communication first. A male sales executive explained to me that one of the things he has always appreciated about his female colleagues was their ability to adapt their communication style to best fit the person that they're trying to influence. He explained, "In sales, getting on your customer's 'communication channel' is key, as it makes it a whole lot easier to explain your value and describe the benefits of your solution in a meaningful way. This can be a big factor in whether the customers want to partner with you or buy your services."

Equally important is communicating effectively with folks inside the organization. Bill Richardson, executive vice president of Global Business Development at PPD (previously CEO of Dow Hickam Pharmaceuticals and CEO of Bertek Pharmaceuticals), shared with me that in less than a decade, the workforce will look quite different, with over half being millennials by the year 2014. Bill said that the members of this "up-and-coming" generation are having a difficult time trusting the company they work for and, in particular, their management team. They have seen so many businesses close, people's retirement accounts blown out of the water, and people with 20 to 30 years of service with a company being tossed by the wayside because of the harsh realities of today's economy.

These millennials are asking more questions and demanding more answers. They want to know what's going on inside the organization, how the company is planning to grow and gain or retain a competitive advantage, and how they personally can add to their experience and skill sets by working for the organization. This calls for communicating on a greater level and more effectively. It also calls for building stronger and more supportive relationships with our teams to connect with their needs, concerns, and career motivations. If we're not being proactive in this respect, we stand a good chance of losing a lot of great talent, because the members of this group are expecting that level of investment. They aren't the generation of the silent majority!

And in terms of collaboration, employees today want to get involved. They want to make a significant contribution and be recognized for their value to the greater good of the organization. They want to participate in meetings, on task forces, and with clients. But they also don't want to waste their time, which means they need to feel that their ideas are heard, understood, and incorporated.

The men we interviewed recognized that women are good at this. Based on their relational approach and ability to integrate both sides of the brain, women naturally can draw out the perspectives of others and then connect the different points of view. This makes people feel validated and appreciated. Collaboration doesn't mean that everything has to drive toward consensus. It just means that people have the opportunity to impact the outcome. And the executives I talked with expressed a sincere appreciation for being able to partner with a woman in order to have her skill set regarding collaboration complement their drive for closure and results.

4. How to Think More Holistically

This actually surprised me. I always thought men went crazy when women wanted to look at the "bigger picture" or "consider all the options." But the executives we surveyed agreed that while it was sometimes irritating in the moment, they recognized that by considering a broader perspective, they often came up with a better solution and avoided potential problems.

Juan C. Jones, senior vice president of Customer Support Services North America at Oracle, said, "One of the important strengths that women bring to my team is having a more holistic and integrated perspective. Being that Oracle has evolved beyond software to engineered systems, we need to be sure that we look at the greater computing system versus just the individual components. If we only look at our business from a left-brain way of thinking (solving the immediate problem), not only can we get caught in the weeds but, more important, we might miss the bigger opportunities. Taking on a more integrated approach to our thinking has allowed us to examine the requirements differently and connect all the different parts of the computing system to provide a complete end-to-end or engineered system. That's really what our customers need—more complete solution thinking. We have a lot of men who are great at dissecting all the individual components of the solution. However, by having a women's integrated perspective, it helps balance our analytical thinking with intuition and really helps us to communicate and strategize with our customers differently."

And I don't think this is only true of IT organizations. We heard similar stories from across the industries. I never asked if finding the value in the holistic view made it any easier to "grin and bear it" in the moment, but I'd like to think it did.

5. How to Trust Your Intuition

Frankly, when we asked about this, we had to define what we meant when we said "intuition." So, just to be clear—we defined *intuition* as "knowing with no evidence." I'm not sure that's what *Webster's* would say, but it's what women understand right away. To be somewhat more scientific, it's what we refer to as our *gut feeling*. And today's research is showing that our intuition is pretty reliable.

One of my favorite examples of this was shared again by Juan C. Jones at Oracle. A woman on his team had been the account manager for one of the company's largest clients for several years. When this client sent Juan a list of concerns and requests, his reaction was to knock off the list and assume that the client would be fine as a result. Maribeth, the account manager, thought that the list was indicative of the client having a bigger issue. When Juan asked her to explain, she said that it just didn't "feel right." She actually convinced him to travel out to see the client to determine what the people there were really thinking and concerned about.

Juan said, "We did and learned that we had a real customer confidence issue. Essentially they wanted to be sure that we were going to be there for them in the long run, that we would take time to understand their strategy, and that we would deliver on our product road map. Once we addressed those concerns, we strengthened our relationship and eventually renewed our long-term partnership. Juan credits Maribeth's intuition not only for saving the client, but also for teaching him a valuable lesson—which was not to rely on his own thinking when dealing with, in this case, a key customer issue, but rather to embrace and tap into the full spectrum of leadership thinking within his team.

Men still represent over 80 percent of the executive suite and corporate board of directors and therefore are an important part of the solution to creating an Integrated Leadership Model. Savvy and successful organizations will find ways to engage men in fostering more balanced leadership teams.

Chapter Summary

- Historically, men have been pushed to the sidelines when it comes to advancing women into the senior ranks and creating balanced leadership teams across the enterprise.
- Women can better engage men by helping them understand how their roles can be helpful by providing their support toward the development and advancement of women.
- Smart men understand the value of gender diversity and know there are many skills they can learn from women, such as:
  - How to be a better listener
  - How to be empathetic
  - How to foster better communication and collaboration
  - How to think more holistically
  - How to trust their intuition

Chapter 6

Men's Biases
About Women

IF MEN VALUE what women bring to the table, what's stopping them from embracing the notion of pulling more talented women into the senior leadership ranks? I believe most male executives have good intentions and want to help more women advance into the senior ranks. The main obstacle is something many men aren't even aware of. The obstacle is their biases, and biases often rule our world!

The definition of *bias* in *Webster's* dictionary is fairly general, "a temperamental or emotional leaning to one side." And like it or not, biases are a fact of life. Yet when I ask men to describe their biases about women, a common response is, "Biases? What biases?" We all have them, both men and women, but it's hard for us to know what they are because they have been hardwired into our nervous system for years, and they reside in our unconscious mind.

Kathy Hannan, national managing partner, Corporate Responsibility and Diversity, with KPMG LLP, shared with me, "Unconscious biases exist in even the most inclusive organizations. It's human nature. But it's what you do with—and about—those biases that counts. Something we need to do more of is training on these *unconscious* biases, and focus on how managers can have a dialogue about them with a higher degree of accountability. If an organization understands the business case for having more women in senior leadership positions, they need to support that by taking clear, consistent, and measurable steps to be sure they don't lose their female talent. It begins with building awareness of unconscious biases across the enterprise, and then training people to help them understand where those biases come from and how they can overcome them. And that includes training every level of leadership. Whatever the reason, companies need to be sure their intellectual capital isn't walking out the door!"

The bottom line of Kathy's message is that gender biases are prevalent and must be addressed. Despite the fact that businessmen have been working closely with women for decades, we haven't made as much progress as many would like in terms of moving beyond some of the old stereotypes that influence how we view a woman's readiness to advance to senior levels. Often our unconscious biases translate into negative assumptions that both men and women make about each other. For example, a common complaint I hear from women is, "Men don't listen." And it's not unusual for a man to say, "Women are too emotional."

Even if we aren't drawing these kinds of erroneous conclusions, we often just plainly misinterpret each other. Let me give you my favorite example of this. Phrases that are commonly used by women include "This may be a silly question but . . . ," "I feel . . . ," "What if we consider . . . ," "Maybe we should . . . ," or "Perhaps we could . . ." While these statements reflect women's relational traits and their intention to build trust and inclusiveness, men often see them as weak, indecisive, lacking confidence, or too emotional.

As we learned from brain research, part of this mistranslation is that women prefer to be relational and men tend to be transactional. The typical result of this disconnect is that in a meeting, when a woman brings up an idea this way, men don't take her as seriously as they would when another man makes the same point differently. It's bad enough that these kinds of interactions can be personally upsetting to a woman, but they may also lower morale and negatively affect overall job satisfaction.

A recent Gallup survey asked 1.7 million men and women in 101 companies in 63 countries whether they felt they "had the opportunity to do their best every day in their job." Believe it or not, only 20 percent of employees said yes. And being able to do our best at work is directly related to how satisfied we are with our work situation. I wonder how many of that 80 percent are impacted by the biases and filters others have about them. We may never be able to measure this single factor, but I would assume the correlation is fairly significant.

Let's take a look at the most common biases that show up when women are being considered for the top jobs and see how we can rewire our thinking.

1. Women Are Too Emotional

I once heard from a male colleague that "Women take care. Men take charge." Well, I'm not sure that's actually true, but if it were, wouldn't it be great if executive teams did both! In terms of being emotional, we know that women score higher on EQ (emotional quotient) tests and that they display considerably more empathy. We also know that the nurture factor is an important leadership trait.

But what does that actually mean for men? For senior managers, it means that since women have a natural capacity for listening and being able to pick up on people's feelings and concerns, an executive team with women will be better able to "walk in someone else's shoes," which in turn helps build stronger customer relationships and foster more cross-collaboration throughout the organization. Sure, men might have to deal with a different kind of sensitivity and talk more about "feelings" than they might like in this type of situation, but it seems to me that this would be a small price to pay in return for such a unique and valuable skill set!

2. Women Don't Have as High Aspirations as Men

The assumption that women lack ambition is just not true. Women are just as driven as men and just as motivated to be rewarded for their hard work and accomplishments. However, the difference between the two is how they define what success looks like.

For men, success tends to be equated with title, money, power, and material things. Women, on the other hand, define success around the relationships they have at work, the knowledge that their subordinates believe and support them, and the opportunity to deliver a quality product or service to their customers. Ironically, while women also want the recognition and rewards associated with their success, they resist self-promotion.

So in order to make a change in the workplace, I am suggesting that we need to be more open and inclusive when it comes to gender differences in terms of career success. Rather than assuming a woman doesn't want to be a CEO, ask her! It could be that she wants the position but for very different reasons than those of a man. For example, it may not be the title, money, or power that many men associate with the role, but the opportunity to make a difference for the customers or foster stronger relationships with their partners and alliances. What's key is to realize and appreciate how individuals view success in their own eyes and not dismiss their aspiration levels because they are not the same as yours.

3. Women Aren't Strategic Enough!

The assumption that women are not strategic is another major reason why many women don't advance to the next level. I think this is a catch-22. Because women are so good at getting things done, based on their ability to multitask along with their strong attention to detail, they are constantly called on to put out fires, take on the most difficult assignments, and deal with the most time-consuming clients—both internally and externally. Having all these responsibilities forces them to remain very tactical for sheer survival. If given the choice, the women I talk with would choose to have a greater impact by setting direction and solving bigger problems. They would love to stop what they are doing long enough to think strategically! And here's the catch: they are recognized for promotion because of what they are able to accomplish—at the tactical level—and then not promoted because they aren't seen as strategic enough.

The only solution I see in the short term is for their managers to provide them with opportunities to focus less on the task and more on bigger-picture issues where they can learn those skills and where they will also have the opportunity to prove to others that they can be strategic.

4. Women Aren't Good Negotiators

No one should ever assume women can't negotiate. A female executive shared that every time her fellow executives (all men) need to negotiate a major deal, they invite her to be a part of the negotiating team. She learned early on when being invited to participate in negotiations that her unique strengths and traits complemented those of her male colleagues. Her collaborative style and acute ability to listen in combination with her male colleagues' data-driven, fact-based approach and "drive-for-results" style made for a successful and better outcome than having the men carry on the negotiations without someone like her to balance out the conversation. According to a Hay Consulting study, women executives tend to foster genuine collaboration, whereas male executives are far more likely to view negotiations and other business transactions as zero-sum games.

Women's natural traits tend to directly relate to some important factors for successful negotiations. They have an innate ability to read signals or unspoken words. By reading the signals in a negotiating process, not only do you know where you stand, but you intuitively surmise how to successfully build rapport and are better able to adapt or modify your approach as needed for achieving a successful outcome.

Also, while it's important for everyone to have all the facts lined up and the business case established before the actual negotiations, a woman's natural skills of collaborating, of listening, and of feeling and showing empathy will help to expand the negotiation into a conversation that will draw out the other parties' fears, concerns, and alternative options, which often leads to the best outcome for a long-term relationship.

5. Women Aren't Risk Takers and Can't Make the Tough Decisions

Okay, I'll give you this one. Women can seem like they avoid risks and want to consider all the options before making a decision. As the brain research tells us, women are wired to think more holistically, while men tend to be more transactional and therefore need less "consideration" when deciding. A male colleague told me that men view problem solving as decisiveness, while women view problem solving as coming up with the right answer. For men, decision making is fairly straightforward, and for women it is more of a process. This explains why women want to explore all the options and even generate multiple solutions. They want to feel comfortable that they've made the best decision. To men, this can be perceived as overcommunicating, or taking too much time and covering too much information—which can be seen as a problem.

In today's complex business environment, at the executive level, it's critical in many situations to take an integrated approach to addressing problems and making important decisions. However, this reluctance to make a decision and the tendency to overthink problems (which I too grapple with) can be self-limiting. It can cause men to think that women aren't strong enough to make the tough decisions. I don't believe this is true, but it certainly seems to be a common male reaction. I believe once a woman is convinced that a decision is the right one, she is very capable of owning and implementing it—no matter how tough it is.

My point is that our assumptions have a tendency to be incorrect, or even if they are partially correct, they can often be viewed differently if we just take the time to really look into them. Let me give you a prime example. I was working with a senior vice president of sales, Steve, who was focused on strengthening his sales management team and was complaining that he didn't have any strong saleswomen who were interested in taking on a management position. I asked about Susan, who was a very successful major account representative and had been highly effective in both finding new business and expanding service in her existing accounts. She had great client relationships and was what I considered to be a prime candidate for a management position. I knew Susan fairly well because I had worked with her on a diversity project the year before. I was impressed by her strong sense of organization and her ability to get all sorts of people—both inside and outside the organization—to speak at a conference we were sponsoring. Steve's idea that no women were interested in a higher position left me very curious.

He said, "Oh, Susan isn't interested in taking on more responsibility. She just got married, and I'm sure she wouldn't want to have more client meetings and events to go to in the evenings. Never mind the extent of travel that is involved in managing an entire territory." My immediate reaction was to wonder if Steve would have made those same assumptions about a male employee. Or would he have thought that a promotion into management would be perfect for a guy who was settling down and taking on more responsibility?

As you can imagine, we had quite a discussion about this, and the result was interesting. Steve realized that he had been making several assumptions about Susan. He had assumed that since she never spoke to him about wanting a promotion, she was content with her role and her income. Wrong! He had also assumed that the sales management role entailed extensive travel because it used to when he was running a territory—before the advent of today's technology. Partially wrong. And finally he had assumed that it would be a difficult decision for her at this particular time. Right, but not for the reasons he thought. It seems that Susan had been offered a sales management position with another company, a company that recognized her value and had not made the same assumptions about her that Steve had made.

When Steve discussed the management position with Susan, it became a negotiation rather than just a discussion! Steve admitted to Susan that he had jumped to some assumptions before checking them out with her and hoped that she would stay with the company. Susan told Steve that the only reason she was looking on the outside was because she felt as though she was being passed by for opportunities she was qualified for; hence she felt as though her abilities were not valued. Steve then asked her to stay with the company, and feeling that she was the best person for the job, he offered her the new sales leadership role that had just opened up. Susan ended up taking the position along with a nice increase in her compensation. Within a year, she was able to outperform her peers in the sales organization—a win for Susan and the company!

Check Your Biases

Since we all come into the workplace with a set of unconscious biases, which translate into preconceived notions about one another, I am going to show you a tool that SHAMBAUGH uses to help both men and women check their assumptions before drawing a conclusion about another individual. To use it, think of a person whom you have formed a preconceived bias or made an assumption about. By that I mean, you think you know something about him or her without actually checking it out. Maybe your opinion is based on prior experience, or what you have heard from others, or even just based on your intuition. Now answer the following questions:

- What exactly is the assumption you are making about this person?
- What are you basing this on? Where does the assumption really come from? Do you have factual evidence to support your assumption?
- What do you think this person would say about your assumption?
- How might your assumption be incorrect?
- How might you check out this assumption to find out if it is true?
- What might be the advantages and disadvantages of investigating your assumptions?
- What positive and negative consequences could there be of looking into your assumptions?

The more we can recognize and address our biases and subsequent assumptions with intentionality, the better we will be able to close the gender gap, tap and leverage gender intelligence, and drive greater levels of employee satisfaction, commitment, and performance. As I mentioned before, women hold more than 50 percent of professional and managerial jobs in the United States. And we can't dismiss the emergence of women from other countries who are also filling those seats. They represent a highly skilled source of leadership talent, and in some cases—as a result of continued biases—they are being overlooked or inadvertently discouraged to the detriment of business success. In today's global and competitive marketplace, those companies that can tap into the talent of both men and women will have an advantage over those that only rely on men filling their top positions.

Chapter Summary

- Most male executives have good intentions and want to help more women advance into the senior ranks. The men's main obstacle to their doing so is their unconscious biases and preconceived notions.
- Some of the most common biases men have about women in senior leadership include:
  - Women are too emotional.
  - Women don't have as high aspirations as men.
  - Women aren't strategic enough.
  - Women aren't good negotiators.
  - Women aren't risk takers and can't make the tough decisions.
- Always check your biases and assumptions before drawing a conclusion about another individual.
- The more that all of us—men and women—can intentionally recognize and address our biases and assumptions, the better we will be able to leverage the gender intelligence within our organizations.

Chapter 7

What Men Aren't Telling Women

I'M SURE IT'S NOT a surprise to anyone that there are conversations that men "at the top" have *about women* that women never hear. These conversations don't take place in meetings or during daily business discussions. Instead, they happen at times and in places where women seem to be absent—like the boardroom, the golf course, or even the men's bathroom!

These conversations are critical for women to know about in order to better understand the male perspective on what it takes to be successful as a senior executive. Once men and women know what each other is thinking, they can begin to check out specific assumptions, better understand each other, and leverage each other's strengths. This deeper understanding will allow them to give each other meaningful advice, as well as support, that will result in men and women working together more synergistically. After all, that's what this idea of Integrated Leadership is all about!

Based on my many hours of interviews, here are just a few of the *doubts* men have about women being able to function at the executive level and *advice* they have (but are often uncomfortable sharing) for women who want to make it to the top.

Work-Life Balance

Men's Concerns. *Can you really do it all? Can you spend the time and energy doing what needs to be done at this senior level and still be the person you want and need to be at home?*

Men at the top recognize that their job can be all consuming. They often sacrifice family time for work, and if they have children, they are grateful that they have someone at home to keep that part of their life in order and to take care of raising the kids. When I talk to male executives about this, they confess that they feel bad missing soccer games and dance recitals, but they are relieved that someone else is there to do it.

A few of the male executives I've worked with have taken the position that they can keep their family as a scheduling priority and still be successful—but these men are *definitely* in the minority. So the majority of male executives have the genuine concern that women who have families just can't put in the time that it takes to do the top jobs. And this concern is magnified when they respect and really care about a woman who is doing a brilliant job and wants to advance in her career. Some actually try to convince these women to keep doing what they are doing—for their own peace of mind and happiness!

Men's Advice for Women. *Be very clear about what you want in your life at this time. Figure out what success looks like to you for the next five years, what price you are willing to pay (both professionally and personally) to achieve that success, and how you can best set your life up today so that five years from now, you can look back and say it was all worth it.*

I work with women to help them address this very issue every day. We work on what I call a personal mission statement that considers things like *What are my personal values? What do I want to be known for? What is most important to me now? What will be important to me 5 years from now? 10 years from now? 20 years from now?* Then we talk about what it will take to achieve those goals—both short and long term. Finally, I help them to develop a plan that will help them to set a direction for themselves and stay on course to reach their goals. It's ironic that we do this exercise all the time in business but so infrequently in our personal lives. Maybe that's why I so often find myself coaching a woman who wants one thing in her life but ends up making choices that get her something very different!

I was actually encouraged recently after speaking to a male executive in a Fortune 500 company who told me that one of his highest priorities was to "be there" for his kids while they were still living at home. He told me that when he is in town, he leaves his office every day at 5:15 so he can have dinner with the family at 6. And he said that when he leaves the office at 3:15 in the afternoon, he doesn't hide the fact that he's going to watch his kid's game at school. He wants to model for his staff that it's OK to set your life up so you can be the person you want to be. It's the results you produce that count, not the time you are "on the job." Now, just to be clear, he also admitted that he often works in the evening, after the kids go to bed, or gets up early in the morning to answer e-mails from around the world, but that's the price he's willing to pay in order to achieve what he considers to be success at work and at home.

I am sharing this story, as I know there are a number of women who are challenged with balancing work and life. I know it's hard. However, this example illustrates that men can also be challenged with work-life issues, but in some ways I think they are better at setting boundaries and not feeling guilty about leaving early to be with the kids or go to that soccer game that your son is playing in. Many women we coach at SHAMBAUGH struggle with this sense of guilt when taking time for themselves—or in this case leaving the office at a reasonable hour to be with their family. In this example, the male executive set expectations early on regarding his work hours and didn't allow himself to get into a pattern where people just expected him to be the last one to turn off the lights.

He also shared a story that showed me that we are making progress on the work-life balance issue for both genders. He said, "We were in one of our performance review meetings when I knew I had some work to do with my staff. We were talking about a very high performer who was being considered for a promotion when one person on my team said, 'I don't know why everyone thinks this guy is so valuable. He leaves here every day at 4:30. How dedicated can he really be?' At first, I found myself smiling when I thought about this guy actually cracking the code for getting balance into his life at such a young age (it took me a lot longer!), but then I heard others in the room actually buying into that skepticism. I listened for a while and then said, 'We should all figure out how this guy does such a great job and still leaves at a decent time, rather than sitting here criticizing him for it. Why are we talking about this as a negative? What does this say about us rather than him?'" What a smart man and enlightened business leader!

Building and Capitalizing on Your Strategic Network

Men's Concerns. *While you are great at relationship building, do you really know the right people both inside and outside your organization that can help us to achieve our goals? Are you an asset to our business in terms of your contacts and your influence with them?*

Men at the top know that much of their success depends on whom they know and what others are willing and able to do for them. They have often spent years building relationships with senior staff in every function of the organization, within their client organizations, and throughout their industry. As a result, these men have a broad business perspective as well as a strong sense of the industry and their competition. They don't hesitate to pick up the phone to set up a business lunch with someone they've only met once or send an e-mail to someone that has been referred to them, asking for information, insights, or assistance. That's what's called strategic networking! And it's a two-way street. They often find themselves responding to the requests of others, knowing that reciprocity is a big part of doing business today.

Men's Advice for Women. *Check your network to be sure you are connected to the right people—those who can help you and your team to be successful. This means having meaningful relationships with your colleagues in all parts of our organization as well as with key decision makers and influencers in your current and potential client organizations. Get to know leaders in your industry so you can continue to grow, become the best in your field, and stay at the top of your game.*

If you've read my book *It's Not a Glass Ceiling, It's a Sticky Floor,* you may recognize this as being one of the greatest challenges for many women. An entire chapter addresses this topic, and while a large portion of that chapter focuses on exactly how to build a strategic network, several pages are devoted to why this kind of network is so important.

Men seem to get this better than women. For example, research conducted by Catalyst, a leading research firm, found that 77 percent of women employees indicated that they believe what drives promotions in their firm is a combination of hard work, long hours, and educational credentials. On the other hand, 83 percent of men indicated that in terms of advancement, who you know counts for a large part of success, or at least counts about as much as how well you do your job! These are two very different perspectives.

Jeffrey Tobias Halter, a prior human resources executive at Coca-Cola, explained to me that he feels that moving up in an organization is really all about using your network effectively. Jeff said, "Women are great at forming friendships but seem to feel that having and leveraging a network—engaging with others to gain information or asking for professional favors that are actually for personal gain—is almost a betrayal of the female trust. Men see this very differently. They have no problem calling on each other and being very straightforward about what they want and why they want it. Women need to be able to do this as well if they want to have the same opportunities as men."

This means that women need to network with a purpose. They have to target key individuals, both inside and outside their organization, and develop relationships that do not need to be friendships, but that are significant enough connections that they can call on these individuals for help when it's needed. To do this, I always suggest that a woman put together an intentional plan. Who are you going to contact by when, and what are you going to talk about? Once you have this plan, which ideally is calibrated with a trusted and respected mentor in your organization, you need to set time on your calendar to do it and then hold yourself accountable for achieving the results you are looking for.

Another note is that women often gravitate to people they feel comfortable talking with rather than reaching out to the people that are important for them to know. Since strategic networks need to be broad, insightful, and influential, women need to get out of their comfort zone once in a while. If you're a woman and you're not sure how to approach someone, think about what you have to offer that person. Would an industry expert be interested in the perspective of your company? Would a client want to know you in order to better understand how your organization might help him to be more successful? Would a peer in another part of your organization recognize that getting to know you better might offer her the opportunity to form an important alliance some day?

The key to building and leveraging your strategic network is being clear about your purpose and mindful about executing your plan.

Visibility

Men's Concerns. *Do you really stand out in this organization? Have you made a uniquely positive impression on me and the other leaders in the organization?*

While many women make it into the ranks of middle management, fewer make it to the executive level and considerably fewer make it to the top positions. Some women (never men!) will argue that the "old boys' network" or the "glass ceiling" is the crux of the problem. Well, I've been noticing recently that the "old boys" aren't so old anymore and that mindsets are gradually changing. When I ask men if their daughters could ever grow up to become the CEO of a major organization, the usual response is, "Of course!" So we're talking about a possibility today that probably didn't exist 50 years ago. And when I ask what might get in the way of that happening for their daughters, they mention things like not getting the right education or not wanting to get into that kind of a rat race.

When I probe further, asking why bright, competent women aren't on their executive teams, visibility seems to come up quite often. So let's take a look at the issue of visibility.

There seems to be considerable regard for a person's visibility, both inside and outside the organization. Employees who are not in contact with the senior staff—and, in many cases, with the CEO, COO, or CFO—often get overlooked in the talent pool for the senior positions. Ironically, people from the outside, who are recognized for their talents—even if only on a résumé—or who come highly recommended by someone who is respected by the hiring team, are often considered more intentionally than internal candidates who aren't as well known or don't have the sponsorship of those who can influence the key decision makers.

It's all about visibility with the right folks at the right time! This is often a problem for women who want to show up as part of a team or who want to ensure that their colleagues and direct reports get the acknowledgment they deserve. They are comfortable letting others get the credit and the visibility. Men are more likely to take the credit that they believe they deserve, get in front of the senior staff as often as possible, and get noticed for specific accomplishments.

Men's Advice for Women. *Think about what you want others to know about you and your accomplishments and be sure you are recognized by the right people for the contributions you are making and the talent that you have. Develop influential sponsors who know your potential and want you to advance. Ask them to help you gain the attention and visibility you deserve.*

Credibility

Men's Concerns. *Do you have the respect and influence it takes to be successful at this level?*

Credibility comes as a result of both experience and results. Most successful women have no problem achieving outstanding results in the projects and initiatives they take on, and they often have a wealth of experience. However, in order to be chosen for the most senior positions, two things need to happen. First, the results that women produce need to have made a major impact on the business. Second, their work experience has to be highly regarded in terms of the functions of the business. This means that women must pick and choose their assignments carefully. Not all parts of the business are created equal in the eyes of those at the top. Marketing and HR are often comfortable places to build a career, but many executives will admit that these functions aren't viewed the same way as operations, P&L, and sales, which have a more direct and measurable impact on the bottom line of the business.

As one executive told me, "You get a lot of street credibility being in operations or P&L since those roles force you to understand the core business issues and enable you to communicate across all lines of management with a more cultivated and strategic perspective." That's the kind of credibility you don't get through a formal education or more generalized business experience, and people at the top know it.

Jeff Halter commented on this challenge for women and said, "If you really analyze where chief executives come from, 40 percent come from finance and 40 percent come from operations or sales. So your CEO pool now is 80 percent of either finance or field people. The odds are stacked against you if you are not experienced in these areas. We know that both women and minorities tend to move into staff roles—head of HR, head of marketing and staff—which will never lead to someone becoming CEO." This is a unique challenge for both men and women who lack the "right" experience.

Men's Advice for Women. *When the opportunity comes to take a position that broadens and deepens your business experience in terms of your overall career advancement, choose wisely. In particular, early on in your career, try to take on a variety of positions and work on a wide range of projects. It's important to gain greater exposure and make contributions to specific and targeted parts of the business to gain the credibility you need for advancement to the senior positions. In addition, when you are interfacing with an executive team, those individuals on the team will value your strategic perspective and respect your input because of your knowledge and exposure.*

I don't want to backtrack, but this issue also relates to strategic networks. The people that women need to know in business are those in finance, sales, operations, supply chain, etc. Building social capital with them is essential for success. They are the people who can provide women with valuable insights, help them understand a different (and often critical) point of view, provide critical support, and help women to most credibly speak the real language of business.

Confidence

Men's Concerns. *Are you strong enough to take on new challenges at this level and to lead others who are as good at what they do as you are?*

Men seem to radiate confidence even if they don't necessarily have the requisite expertise or experience. Women, on the other hand, are more likely to be aware of the risks involved in certain situations and prefer to be aware and competent before assuming that they will succeed. And they often share these feelings openly with others. This is seen by men as a lack of confidence. Male business leaders often wonder if they should promote a competent woman when she "lacks confidence," or if they do promote her, they assume that she will gain the necessary confidence once she is in the new position.

Confidence is also seen by men as part of risk taking, and men are generally more eager to take risks with less hesitation than women are. As I mentioned earlier, this may be a result of a woman's Whole Brain® Thinking style, which causes her to take more time to think through all the different concerns, potential challenges, and ultimate results. This kind of additional analysis can get in the way of some women taking on stretch assignments or working in a new area that is outside their comfort zone for fear of failure.

Men's Advice for Women. *Be more willing to take more prudent risks in your career and keep your self-doubts to yourself. "Fake it until you make it" is not a negative piece of advice!*

Bill Richardson, executive vice president of Global Business Development at PPD, shared with me, "The only way you grow is to lose some battles along your way to winning the war. When taking on new opportunities or working in unfamiliar areas where you have little or no experience, it's important to be okay with knowing that you are going to stumble and fall. You will certainly make mistakes, but in the long run you will learn and grow, which will make you considerably more valuable to others. Women need to keep putting themselves out there and taking the risks involved with something that's new to them. But doing this starts with believing in themselves. Women have to know that they can be successful without having all the answers and they have to be willing to fail in order to ultimately succeed."

I want to add that while it's essential for women to let others know that they are ready, able, and willing to take on the tough assignments and to show that they have the confidence that's needed to do a great job, it's also important that women aren't afraid to reach out and ask for help along the way.

Another important part of this equation is that women must be open to feedback from those they trust and respect. It doesn't show a lack of confidence to ask others what they think of your ideas and decisions. And be sure not to only ask for feedback from your fans—sometimes those who are critical of you can give you a different and vital perspective on a situation that will ultimately affect your outcome.

Steve Reinemund, prior chairman of the board of PepsiCo and now dean of business at Wake Forest University, commented to me, "Women need to have a variety of mentors who will give them honest feedback as well as helpful insights. They need to listen and take the feedback to heart. Most of the time that same feedback has some truth to it and could be extremely helpful."

Fitting In

Men's Concerns. *Will you be as comfortable dealing with a male-centered group as you are working with other women? How will your presence affect the current dynamics of this male team?*

This is a topic that is hardly ever acknowledged, and yet when I interview male executives and I bring it up, they reluctantly admit that it is a concern. It's one that they wish they didn't have. In fact, they find it embarrassing to admit, but they know how men talk and deal with each other—what's practically the norm for their behavior—and they fear that women won't be comfortable with it. The bottom line is that they don't want to have to deal with that kind of gender-related conflict. They don't want a woman to be uncomfortable while, at the same time, they don't want to have to ask men to change their behavior in order to accommodate a woman on the team.

While I don't think this is generally a problem when a woman joins an all-male executive team, I understand the concern that a woman might not "fit in" or be able to "go with the flow." When I speak at conferences and leadership forums, it's pretty obvious to me that women tend to talk to each other in small groups and even choose to sit together. This is not to say that men don't do the same thing, but they aren't trying to break into a female-dominated executive group!

Men's Advice for Women. *Make it a point to work in a group that comprises mostly men and take notice of the group dynamics. Get comfortable talking with men about things that interest them. Seek them out and practice making a contribution to their conversation. Watch how they naturally interact with each other so that you won't be surprised when they act that way in other business situations.*

Bill Richardson and I had a great discussion about this. We agreed that the men and women who most impressed us were those who could float around a room and comfortably engage with individuals and small groups. These individuals showed a keen interest in a wide range of conversational topics and were willing to express their own ideas and opinions very naturally.

My advice to women who find this difficult to do is to spend more time intentionally participating in activities and events that men find interesting. This doesn't mean that women need to watch football all weekend, but it is useful to know the scores of particular teams and to even join a fantasy football league if that's what the men in the organization are talking about. The purpose of doing this is to develop a comfort level with topics that are of interest to many men; it will only help you in the end.

I have even gone so far as to suggest to some women that they take up golf. I can't tell you how much business I've uncovered or nurtured with guys on the links! Not because I'm a great golfer (although at this point, I can pretty much hold my own!), but because it gives me an opportunity to relate to men in a variety of different situations. It gives me an opportunity to learn what's important to them, what's of interest to them, and how to have a conversation with them that will resonate when we are back at work. As a result, I'm very comfortable being the only woman in a boardroom filled with men, and I think they are equally comfortable with me.

Chapter Summary

- Men are a valuable source of advice and wisdom for women wanting to advance in the leadership pipeline.
- Here are some of the most common concerns men have about women in senior leadership roles and the advice they would give women about each:

Issue	Men's Advice for Women
Work-life balance	Get clear about what you want in your life and what success looks like to you.
Building a strategic network	Network with a purpose to develop relationships with key people who can help you and your team be successful.
Visibility	Develop relationships with key sponsors who know your value and your contributions.
Credibility	Take positions and projects that broaden and deepen your business experience.
Confidence	Take prudent risks, keep self-doubt to yourself, and "fake it until you make it."
Fitting in	Study male group dynamics and practice making a contribution to the conversation.

Chapter 8

Coaching Women
Off Their Sticky Floors

IN MY EXPERIENCE working with organizations, I have found that men are not as comfortable mentoring women as they are other men. Socially, men are wired to work with men. Let's face it—there are inherent gender differences that make it more challenging to build cross-gender relationships. And in today's hypersensitive workplace, men are much more cautious in their dealings with women. However, when 50 percent of the workforce is made up of women, it behooves men to build bridges, look for women's strengths, and learn how to leverage them. Mentoring women in the leadership pipeline represents a huge opportunity for male executives to grow the company.

Men often ask me how they can help a woman rise to the top by coaching or mentoring her. I usually hand them my *Sticky Floors* book. Understanding women's Sticky Floors—the core beliefs, assumptions, and behaviors women have that often hold them back from achieving their ultimate career goals—is helpful in deciding how to best coach them. Many of these Sticky Floors relate directly to the concerns men have about women advancing to the top as well to the advice they already want to give them. And some of the Sticky Floors are also the inherent strengths of men. For example, being included in informal networks and asking for what you want are both ideal topics for men to coach women about since they seem to do them both more naturally anyway.

Let me share a personal example with you. When I was working in the corporate world early in my career, I was asked to take on a new role that I really wasn't qualified to do. My internal voice said that I didn't have enough experience in that area and that it was a pretty major leap in terms of responsibility and compensation level. It would be a big stretch for me—and one that I might really mess up. In fact, as I was considering it, several of my women colleagues reached out to me and discouraged me from taking it. They said that I had a great job now and that everyone thought I was fantastic at what I did. They didn't understand why I would want to do something else and thought I should stay put and enjoy where I was—which was a very good place to be at my young age.

I had just about decided to take their advice when one of my male colleagues took me out to lunch and gave me another way of looking at it. Tom basically encouraged me to take the job. He said, "You won't know everything when you start out, and you'll make a few mistakes along the way. But there will be people there to help you, and you'll learn as you go. And what's the worst thing that can happen? If this job doesn't work out or if it's not a good fit long term, look at it as a set of new experiences that will create other opportunities for you." He also mentioned that he thought I was being groomed for advancement.

I wound up taking the new job, and Tom was right. I did make a few mistakes in the beginning, but with his coaching and support, I grew in terms of my functional knowledge and my political insights. I also gained the visibility I needed to move into a senior role a year later!

This is just one example of where a man not only can offer a woman a different perspective, but he can also offer insights and advice that come as a result of business conversations women often aren't privy to. While the women advising me were very supportive, they also tended to show their support through concern for my feelings; and in most cases, they kept the conversation channeled within our network of women.

Tom, on the other hand, suggested that the risk was worth the reward and offered to leverage his political capital and connections within the company to support me in succeeding in this new opportunity. He also encouraged me to think differently about myself by pushing through my doubts and my need to be perfect. In many ways, Tom was suggesting that I buck up and stop overthinking the decision. He emphasized that people believed in me and knew I could do the job. He focused on how the political system worked and, as my sponsor, how he could use his credibility and circle of influence to gain broader support and advocacy for me.

The biggest lesson I learned in this situation is that while I should embrace my female network, it's also important to be open to a man's perspective and know that men have good intentions, even if their style and approach is different from mine. Men and women bring different strengths to the mentoring and sponsorship role. This disposition reinforces the body of brain research we talked about earlier that suggests men thrive more in a competitive hierarchical environment and focus more on getting to a bottom-line solution. On the other hand, women tend to focus more on listening to others and taking part in the empathetic and nurturing side of decision making.

Women, if you are clear about what you need and how men can help you, reach out to them. However, if you are vague about your request or don't exhibit a sense of confidence and a "can-do" attitude, the men may feel that supporting and coaching you is not worth their time. So be clear up front about what you are trying to do, why you are seeking their help, and exactly what you want them to do for you. Then be open to what they have to say and curious about what you can learn from them. Before entering into a mentoring relationship, I suggest you read my book and identify your Sticky Floors.

Men, if you are mentoring or have agreed to mentor a woman, you need to understand which Sticky Floors are holding this particular woman back.

Coaching Ideas for Women's Sticky Floors

Work-Life Balance

It truly is hard for some women to be both the person they want to be with their family and the person they want to be at work. Primarily it's all about how they need to spend their time. They don't have enough hours in the day (which often goes into the wee hours of the night!) to get everything done.

One thing you can do to coach a woman who is struggling with this is to help her determine where, at work, she can push back on requests for her time. You can also help her understand how to effectively stick to her priorities in order to spend her time and energy doing what's most important and urgent to get the results she is looking for. This often means saying no to folks who think what they want is also critical and urgent! Women who want to please others will sacrifice their own wants and needs in order to satisfy the wants and needs of others. Giving these women permission to push back and helping them talk through exactly how to say no in politically correct terms and how to negotiate for relief are significant topics for a meaningful discussion.

Perfectionism

Good, better, best / Never let it rest / Until your good is better and your better is best! That pretty much sums up the drive some women have to be perfect in everything they do. Women with this issue truly struggle to understand the concept of "good enough." They often set standards for themselves and their teams that are higher than necessary and even higher than expected. As a result, they have the ultimate fear of letting go and can be viewed by others as micromanaging. As a woman moves up the ladder in an organization, this can become a serious obstacle.

If you are managing a high-potential woman who is struggling with this Sticky Floor, one thing you can do, which might be counter-intuitive at points but I promise it will work in the end, is to expand her range of responsibility. Give her enough people to manage and enough projects to lead or supervise that she has to both trust and rely on others to get the work done and done well.

I had a colleague who worked at GE back in the days when GE was going through significant change. She went from having 6 direct reports to having 17! When she asked Jack Welch how she was ever going to know what each of her staff was doing, his response was that she wouldn't. She would have to pick the right people, give them the right tools, remove obstacles for them, check in periodically to see if they were on track, and then trust that they would do a good job. It worked!

She was forced to set realistic standards and hold people to them, nothing more and nothing less. And she was often pleasantly surprised that people did exceed her expectations, and they did it because they chose to, not because she was micromanaging them.

Loyalty

Some women stay in one job or with one boss longer than they should in regard to their career advancement. They often do this because they like what they are doing and are very successful. Oftentimes these women are high performers, and their manager, whom they like, respect, and enjoy working with, finds them irreplaceable. This combination feels so right, it's hard to imagine that it's wrong! But as a result, a woman can actually stop learning and growing, miss out on greater visibility, and not get recognized for her greater value to the business. She can be easily overlooked when it comes to filling higher positions in other parts of the organization.

These women often believe that if they stay doing an outstanding job, they will eventually get recognized and promoted. As we know all too well, that's not the way it works! As her coach, you might help her to see the disadvantages of staying in one place too long and help her lose her fears about making a change. Here are a few questions that you can use in a coaching session:

- What is keeping you in your current position, with your current boss?
- What can happen short and long term if you take a new position?
- What other positions interest you? What else would you like to know about other parts of this business? How can I help you to explore new possibilities?
- If there is another position open, what might you gain by taking it? What might you lose by not taking it?
- If you take another position and it doesn't work out, what are some contingency plans that will make it easier for you to move forward?

Strategic Networking

Women many times have a lot of good friends but have failed to build relationships with key individuals, inside and outside their organization, who can help them achieve their work and career goals. These same women have connected with people based on circumstances rather than a focused plan. As a result, their network is fairly random and based on friendship rather than on mutual value to each other.

If the woman you are coaching would benefit from expanding and focusing her network, you might coach her to start by forming what

I call her own personal "board of directors." These are folks she can trust to give her an objective view of her strengths and opportunities for improvement, who can help her to build and navigate an energizing career plan, and who can help her determine who else should be in her network—people who will help her achieve success on particular projects as well as help her see a wide range of career opportunities. Then you can introduce her to those particular folks you know would be good for her to have on her board. By doing this, you will be coaching, mentoring, and sponsoring her!

Politically Savvy

Being politically savvy is sometimes easier for men than for women. Some women even associate it with what people do who are controlling, self-serving, dishonest, and even fake. Instead, I believe that being politically savvy essentially boils down to two key things:

1. Always having sources for timely, reliable information and for getting the inside scoop.

2. Knowing who your go-to people are for talking up the information you want disseminated and for garnering the support you want for your positions and initiatives.

With these key points in mind, if you want to coach someone who has this as an issue, try discussing these questions:

- How are decisions made in your business, who are the key decision makers, and who ultimately influences those folks?
- Where do certain individuals stand on particular issues and challenges?
- What is valued and respected in relation to career advancement in your company?

- What projects, meetings, and events should be considered in order to gain more visibility?
- If you attend the same meeting, what did you learn from "reading between the lines" or from someone's nonverbals? Who could you tell was aligned with someone else's position, and how did you pick up on that bit of information?
- What is your perception of executive presence, and how does the person you are coaching score in that area? What is working for her, and what can she improve?
- What is her "personal brand," and how does that measure up to what she wants it to be? What do you think it should be in order for her to advance to the highest levels?

Communication

Women often feel that when they speak up, men don't give them the attention and respect they deserve, and they don't get the results they want. I call this *Making Your Words Count*. If you think back to what I shared about the differences in how men and women process information and how this impacts their communication styles, it is evident that a man's perspective on this issue can be invaluable to a woman who is looking to make it into the boardroom.

If you are coaching a woman on this particular Sticky Floor, you might talk about how to most effectively plan what you are going to say to a male-centered group, how to keep it succinct, and how to stay on task. While women are often comfortable being indirect and subtle, most men respond better to the direct and confident approach. While women often make statements with questions, men can see this as weak and even wishy-washy. In coaching a woman, you might observe her in action and give her feedback about what you thought was positive and what you thought was negative.

If she is speaking to the members of a group in order to influence them, you might discuss what she needs to do with key individuals to "grease the skids" before she actually presents her ideas to the group. Gaining agreement in a group is not always about making your words count in one particular discussion—it's a process, and you can help to better understand this.

Asking for What She Wants

It's not uncommon for a woman to fight hard for her team and even for a specific individual who she thinks isn't getting something he or she deserves or needs. But it seems to be more difficult for women to ask for what they want or need for themselves. This shows up in a variety of situations. Men are more likely to ask for a signing bonus, a particular position or project, or a vacation at an inopportune time. Many women would never do this, but instead they feel that men should recognize what a woman deserves and provide it to her without her having to ask for it!

If you are coaching a woman who deserves or needs something but is not comfortable asking for it, encouraging her in this area can give her the courage to ask in a way that makes it more likely for her to be successful.

You can coach her by helping her:

- Reexamine her worth if she is looking for a promotion or a raise
- Research the validity of her request (industry statistics or prior examples are always good input) so that she has concrete data for comparison
- Build a bridge between her request and the concerns and interests of those involved in the decision

- Figure out what she knows, what she needs to know but doesn't, and how she can get additional information to build a stronger case
- Build a strategy for making the request and a backup plan in case the answer is no
- Feel comfortable in making the request

For decades, men have advocated for other men. But men can also be exceptional advocates for women advancing to senior leadership positions. If we want to create truly balanced and Integrated Leadership teams, we need to tap into their insights, coaching, and mentoring as well as their goodwill.

Chapter Summary

- Mentoring women in the leadership pipeline represents a huge opportunity for male executives to grow the company.
- Many of women's Sticky Floors are also men's inherent strengths and as such represent areas in which men can effectively coach women:

Women's Sticky Floors	Men's Coaching Strategy
Work-life balance	Help her identify priorities and develop strategies to stick to them.
Perfectionism	Give her enough people and projects to manage that she must rely on others to get the work done.
Loyalty	Help her to see the disadvantages of staying in one place or position too long.
Strategic networking	Encourage her to form her own personal board of directors.
Political savvy	Show her how to develop sources for getting the inside scoop and garnering support.
Communication	Help her to plan what she will say, how to keep it succinct, and how to stay on message.
Asking for what she wants	Help her to see the validity of something she deserves or needs.

Chapter 9

What Men Can Do to Help Women Advance

So what can men do to help achieve more gender-related balance on their senior leadership teams? Pull more talented women into the executive suite since the men are already there, of course!

So far, we have talked about the two significant ways to help women advance:

1. **Identify and assess your biases about women.** Using the assessment tool in Chapter 6, answer the questions for the individual women you work with. How are your biases affecting your working relationships with these women?

2. **Be proactive about coaching, mentoring, and sponsoring talented women.** Women feel comfortable asking other women for coaching and mentoring but don't feel as comfortable asking men. They are sometimes afraid they will appear weak or less competent. They know men are competitive and are vying for advancement themselves, which sometimes makes asking for their help awkward. I also find that many women don't really know what to ask for. Even when a man offers to help, women aren't specific enough in

terms of their requests, which leaves a man feeling unsure of how he can actually help.

To truly make a difference, take on the personal goal of helping at least one very talented woman in your company to be even more successful or to gain the visibility and credibility she deserves to advance to the senior ranks of leadership. Select this woman carefully, and when you do, be clear about your intention and put a plan together that you will commit to.

There are also a few other things men can do. My additional suggestions are going to sound pretty basic and, on the surface, even easy—but don't be fooled, they aren't basic at all. If they were, more men would be doing them!

You see, after interviewing over 50 male executives for this book, I discovered that most men don't know how to initiate these kinds of conversations with women or even how to build relationships with women who don't share their interests. They can "talk shop" with them all day long, but when it comes to dealing with a woman's personal issues, challenges, concerns, dreams, aspirations, or requests, it seems that men just aren't comfortable doing it. In addition, they also tell me that they don't know how to talk to their male peers about their concern about the lack of women in the senior ranks without sounding like they're putting men down.

Well, if you are feeling uncomfortable talking about women advancing in the workplace, here's my advice:

- **Find your comfort zone for reaching out to help women.** Find ways to seek out high-performing women (throughout your organization) who can work on projects with you and then use this work association as an opportunity to get to know them better. Find out what interests them and what they enjoy doing. Talk about the kind of work they would ultimately like to be doing as well as their career advancement aspirations.

If you feel that they have potential and that you can help them to advance, ask them how you might help them. One man I interviewed told me that he feels pretty comfortable now saying, "How can I help you to be successful? How can we work together so we are both successful? What can you gain from me, and what can I learn from you?" Setting up the situation as a mutually beneficial relationship seems to work well for him. He has coached several women into the vice presidential ranks and one to senior vice president, and so I think he knows what he's talking about!

- **Bring more women into the fold.** If you are in a position to select individuals for a senior leadership team, consider having more than just one woman on it. Too often, I find that the talented women in a company are sprinkled across the organization, each fighting to secure her equal spot on a male-dominated leadership team. This is especially true with the senior leadership teams in Fortune 500 companies. It's like we have the token women heading up HR or marketing, but seldom do I find a woman who is heading up sales or operations. Really now, what's that about? Can you imagine being the only male on the team? The conversations might center on very different topics, and solving problems and making decisions might be handled in a very different way from how you're accustomed to interacting with each other—and how comfortable would all that be for you? When at least two women are on the team, they garner more support and have a greater impact. That's just a fact of group dynamics! Even very strong salmon must get tired of swimming upstream all the time!

  What if you aren't in a position to staff leadership teams? My advice is that you should at least try to make the few women on your team feel more comfortable. Note how other men on the team are paying attention to what a woman is saying. If they aren't giving her the attention and respect she deserves, step in and call them out on their behavior. Actively bring women into the discussion if they are being reticent or ignored. Look for the diversity of thought and appreciate a different perspective. And if a guy "goes off" on a woman, call him on his inappropriate behavior. Stand up for her and make the team a challenging but safe place for everyone.

Karen Dahut, senior vice president at Booz Allen Hamilton, points out, "I think there are two critical things men can do to support a better balance. First, men need to recognize that their voice really matters, and they need to invite women in. Just the simple act of saying, 'Hey, Karen, what do you think?' is so important. Second, they need to be willing to take risks on people they don't know. Naturally, they are going to know the guys better. But they need to be willing to take some risks on people they don't know as well, such as women and men who aren't like them."

- **Use an appreciative approach to leadership with women on your team.** If you aren't familiar with Appreciative Leadership, it involves solving problems by finding and focusing on what is already working and then applying those same elements to be more successful in another area or with a different problem. The important idea here is to recognize an individual's strengths and build on them to help them be more successful in different areas and to ultimately advance in their career. This step works with both men and women, but it's especially powerful in working with women.

- **Give women constructive feedback.** Some men are hesitant or cautious about giving women constructive feedback. Studies show that a majority of men will withhold negative feedback from women because of the fear that they may inadvertently hurt their feelings or that they will be perceived as harassing them. Yet women need this kind of feedback just as much as men do. Unfortunately, that's the downside to affirmative action plans and the litigious society we live in today. When speaking with women, it's important not only to provide honest feedback, supportive guidance, and helpful tips, but also not to sugarcoat the key message. If there is something a woman, or man, needs to do to improve or do differently, you need to make your point in order to be effective. If you do it professionally and with the right intention, you'll be fine!

Mary Fontaine, who works as a business consultant for Hay Consulting, said that, ironically, as women become more visible when they move up in the organization, they also become more isolated, and they don't get the kind of feedback that they need to most effectively manage themselves and their career. She noted, "I think women at the top need to do a better job of seeking constructive feedback. Without feedback, women don't have the ability to adjust their behavior and improve their performance. Highly visible women who don't perform or who don't meet job expectations are easily stigmatized and often never find out exactly what happened. Men need to have both the courage to speak up and the ability to provide meaningful feedback constructively."

Joyce Mullen, vice president of Global Alliances and Global OEM Solutions for Dell, agrees with this. She shared with me that:

Honest, constructive, and direct feedback is an amazing gift. As leaders, the most helpful coaching we can provide to a colleague or team member, male or female, is this direct feedback, supported by examples.

For the feedback to be effective, it has to be heard. Ask your colleagues or team members for their ideas on how to address the issue. This tactic helps confirm that the message is getting through. If you are unsure of how you are performing as a leader on giving feedback to women, bring in a third party (coach, colleague, mentor, direct-line manager, HR professional) to observe, test, and make suggestions on how to improve your coaching skills.

To Joyce's point, there is a skill in giving feedback. It takes one's full attention to not only be aware of the situation, but also provide feedback in such a way that it is constructive and does not put the person on the defensive, so that both parties can jointly work together through the issue.

If you're not familiar with how to give constructive feedback, here's a quick review: Explain what you have noticed (observation) and describe what impact it seems to have had. Be specific and give examples. Then pause and listen to the person's response. If she mentions what you wanted to discuss, build on her response; if not, move the conversation forward by asking her permission for you to share your thoughts. Then provide helpful advice and offer your support.

Today's progressive male leaders know that Integrated Leadership is the way to go—that it is the leadership model that will be required for success in the future. They also clearly understand that they can help their organizations and teams achieve it by doing everything they can to help more women advance and succeed.

Chapter Summary

- The two primary ways men can help women advance are to identify their own biases about women and be more

proactive about coaching, mentoring, and sponsoring
talented women.

- There are also other things men can do to help achieve more
gender-balanced leadership teams:
    - Seek out high-performing women throughout the
    organization to work on projects with you and get to
    know these women better.
    - Bring more women into the fold if you are in a position to
    select individuals for a senior leadership team.
    - Use an appreciative approach with women on your team
    by focusing on what is already working for them and then
    applying those same elements to a different area or
    problem.
    - Give women constructive feedback with supportive
    guidance but don't sugarcoat the message.

Part II Summary

This segment of the book emphasizes the importance of inviting men to be a part of the solution for developing and advancing the women in their organization. For years we have unintentionally kept men to the sidelines when the reality is their experience, perspective, and feedback can be extremely helpful for women to further advance their own leadership. Not only can women benefit from the support of men but men can benefit from women's insights, skills, and thinking. To achieve balanced leadership that is fully integrated we need to be aware and address our own biases. When we do, that naturally sets the foundation for tapping into the broader spectrum of gender intelligence, which leads to enhanced innovation, employee engagement, and decision making—all contributing to better business performance. Here are some practical tips and best practices to help men be a champion for helping the women on their team and across the organization tap their full potential and advance to the senior levels of leadership.

Part III

Integrated Leadership:
Women's Role

Chapter 10

Misconceptions Women Have About Being an Executive

IN PART II, we discussed the role of men in fostering Integrated Leadership. Now, in Part III, we will address women's roles and responsibilities for creating a gender-balanced leadership approach and provide specific strategies, tools, and techniques for raising women's personal leadership quotient so that they can rise to higher positions.

Much of the conventional wisdom about why there aren't more women in the senior leadership ranks is based on the premise that "the system" is stacked against them or there is something wrong with the system. While there may legitimately be some obstacles that keep women from achieving their career goals, I believe, for the most part, that women hold *themselves* back. They are often their own worst enemy in this respect. A glass ceiling may still exist in some organizations, but most women are stuck on a Sticky Floor of self-limiting assumptions, beliefs, and behaviors that prevent them from realizing their potential and moving to the next level of leadership.

In my book *It's Not a Glass Ceiling, It's a Sticky Floor*, I defined and illustrated the Sticky Floors concept for women who are in midrange management positions. It makes sense to now explore the things that hold women back from more senior positions. As I noted in an earlier chapter, I call these "Sticky Floors 2.0," and they involve a completely different set of challenges, opportunities, and dynamics from the Sticky Floors I addressed in my first book. In these next few chapters, my goal is to challenge the thinking and assumptions of women who feel "stuck" at work or frustrated with their inability to advance to the senior level. I think you'll find it fascinating and even humorous what we women tell ourselves with little or no evidence and how we weave our self-talk into self-limiting webs.

In order to take a seat at the executive leadership table and create a truly Integrated Leadership team, women must look within themselves and determine what they are doing (or not doing) that is holding them back, and then they need to map out a plan to achieve what exactly they define as success in their careers. They must assume responsibility for their own career advancement and adapt their beliefs, assumptions, and behaviors accordingly. In most cases, if women will take the time to objectively look at themselves and have the courage to make changes, they can have more choices and access to better opportunities.

To begin, let's look at the false assumptions many women have about executive leadership. Believe it or not, there are a number of myths that women believe about moving up the leadership pipeline, and in many cases these false assumptions have prevented them from taking their career to the next level. Many of SHAMBAUGH's clients tell us that they can't get their women to the level of senior vice president. This is a real concern for them because it directly impacts their growth capabilities. It's not that women lack competence or experience. Rather, it seems that many women have assumptions—some correct and some incorrect—about what it's like to work at the executive level, and those assumptions discourage them from wanting to move in that direction. These assumptions can evolve into myths that can negatively impacting the career decisions of very talented women.

In conducting research for this book, I had the opportunity to interview a number of accomplished women executives who shared their experience with myths about working in the senior ranks and also explained why certain myths are simply not true. Some admitted that at some point in their career they had actually put more emphasis on these false assumptions about being an executive than they did on the benefits—which range from having greater influence to making significantly more money.

A common theme that all the women executives shared with me was that once they advanced to more senior levels, their preconceived assumptions about being an executive, or that voice inside saying they were not qualified to do the job, were only self-limiting obstacles that never came true. If they had allowed these false assumptions to take over their decision-making process regarding the next job, it would have prevented them from reaching new heights and success in their career and life. They learned that the benefits and opportunities presented outweighed the negatives and that some of the negatives never came true. There are always going to be fears and concerns when trying on something different from or bigger than what you are used to, but many of these turn out to be myths that never unfold.

The Six Most Common Myths About Women Moving into the Senior Executive Ranks

Myth #1. Executives Are Born Leaders

While some people show innate leadership traits and abilities at a young age, if you look at the executives currently running organizations, you will find that they have a wealth of varied experience and have actually honed their leadership skills on every rung of the corporate ladder as they moved up to the executive suite.

Leadership can be learned—just ask those who are in the military. The military has been developing leaders for generations through a systematic process. We in business need to take the same view: Everyone has the potential to be a leader. The key is to find people who want that role and then give them the knowledge, skills, and experiences that will enable them to develop their leadership potential.

There is no one set of predictors for successful leaders. They come from all socioeconomic groups as well as ethnic backgrounds, and they are both men and women. Some executives are quiet, whereas others are more forcefully vocal; some are technical or functional experts, whereas others have a broad knowledge of organizational dynamics; and some have MBAs, whereas others have plain-old "street smarts."

All the leaders I know will tell you that they learned valuable lessons with every new assignment, challenging project, and politically charged situation. My advice to women has always been to take advantage of every learning opportunity, to volunteer to take on the tough assignments, and to watch what the successful leaders in the business are doing that sets them apart from others. Most organizations have a set of leadership competencies identified for their business, and these can be used as a road map to the executive suite. And don't forget that many of the natural strengths that women possess, such as emotional intelligence, collaborative style, creativity, and integrated thinking, are the "in-demand" traits for today's successful leaders.

Myth #2. In Order to Get a Promotion, I Just Need to Do My Job Exceedingly Well

This is such a female view of the world. And it's not totally incorrect; it's just very misleading. When you do a great job, you get appreciated for that particular activity or deliverable, but not necessarily for your versatility or potential. In fact, your brilliance can actually work against you! It's not fair, but when you set yourself up to be the go-to person for something, you also become indispensable—but only at that level. People who count on you, especially those who are looking to advance leaders in the organization, can feel that they will be at risk if they don't have you still working in that particular capacity—especially if it is vital to their success.

Another unfair part of this equation is that you are often so busy doing what you're doing so well that you don't have the opportunity to gain the visibility with other executives and within other parts of the business. In order to have your reputation brought into the conversation when promotions are being discussed, you need to reach out to others and ensure you have the right people around you who will be your champion and advocate for you when you are not in the room. And I'm sure you have heard, "It's not *what* you know but *who* you know that gets you in the door." The same is true with moving leaders through the pipeline and into the executive ranks.

Kay Kapoor, prior managing director and chief executive at Accenture Federal Services, shared with me that based on her own personal experience and perspective, when it comes to getting promoted, it's all about driving the right kind of results that will gain visibility with the right people. Kay said, "I often hear from women that they are not appreciated or understood. I firmly believe that if you drive the right results, you will, in most cases, get the respect you deserve. No one can argue with great results. Women need to step up and accept those roles that are highly visible and have a significant impact on the business so that they will be noticed for their contribution and have their results taken seriously." She continued, "What I have also learned in terms of getting ahead, particularly in the executive ranks, is the importance of taking time to get to know and work with the senior executives. It's essential to position yourself so they know you. And remember, when you get to that level in an organization, good performance is in some ways 'a given,' so the relational component becomes even more important."

What Kay is saying makes sense. Of course, you need to do a good job. But that's just the beginning in terms of career advancement. In and of itself, doing your job exceedingly well will just get you more of the same work to do. To advance, you have to be able to effectively socialize and leverage your successes. You need a successful track record *and* the appropriate visibility.

Myth #3. I Need to Be Part of the "Old Boys' Network" to Be Selected as an Executive

I have to admit that this might have been true as recently as a decade ago when there were not as many women in the succession pool and, frankly, not as many women interested in the senior positions. But now the landscape has changed significantly, and many more women are getting the right education and experience to advance to the highest levels. Once you're at the middle management level in most organizations, it doesn't matter who you are. What are important are your skills, abilities, and talents along with your accomplishments and your business relationships with the CEO and other executives. And the good news here is that all the research that's been done on high performers indicates that while there might be some style differences among highly successful people, there really aren't performance differences based on gender. So if you are prepared and get the right recognition (from the right people) for your talents and contributions, you can go head-to-head with anyone.

Another piece of this myth is that to be successful as an executive in a male-dominated work environment—which is still a fact in many industries—you have to act like a man to be accepted. Not true. CEOs and other successful business leaders are realizing that the value of having a woman's perspective, as well as her unique skill set and personal traits, is lost if she performs like "just one of the guys." So women may now be wearing pants to work, but they are recognized for their unique contributions that are often in contrast to that of their male counterparts.

Myth #4. Women Are Supportive and Helpful Advocates for Each Other

Based on the assumption that women value trusting and supportive relationships, one might think women executives would be the strongest advocates for other women. Generally speaking, however, we have found this not to be true. And research seems to back this up. One particular study reported that 54 percent of the women surveyed said that other women had never helped them advance in their career, and 9 percent said that women had deliberately held them back.

At SHAMBAUGH, we find in our coaching and leadership programs that some women won't take the time to help other women or simply don't see it as their role to help other women with their careers. We often refer to these women as "queen bees." These are women who have made it to the top and don't necessarily want other women to join them. Perhaps they think there isn't enough room at the top for more women and feel threatened and thus are unwilling to bring others along. Or maybe they believe, "I had to pay my dues. No one made it easy for me. I made it on my own, so they can do the same. Why should I make it easy for someone else?"

While I have always had a community of women who have been supportive and connected me with opportunities, what I hear within my client organizations is that it is easier to tap into senior men within an organization than to reach out to and receive help from senior women. If this is in fact the case, then women are defeating themselves. Many women point to the old boys' network as a reason they can't get ahead (see Myth #3), and yet it seems that women are refusing to start an "old girls' network." Why would we neglect our own power and influence?

One of the best ways to further the development of women—and enhance the success of our organizations—is to reach out and bring other women up. Particularly in the current economy, companies cannot afford to ignore 50 percent of the population when seeking the best talent. Why then, from a business perspective alone, would women executives not mentor and support other women? An Integrated Leadership approach will be required for organizations to operate fully and globally, and that means there will be ever-increasing opportunities for women to rise to senior leadership. So there is plenty of room and opportunities for us all!

Myth #5. There Are No Real Benefits of Being an Executive—Just More Hard Work!

Yes, it is hard work! There's no question that your role as an executive will be demanding in terms of time and energy. Being an executive is a big responsibility—to the employees who rely on your good judgment to provide them with a job, to the peers who team with you to grow the business in the face of unbelievable competition, and to the key stakeholders who have put their trust in you to build a meaningful future for the business.

But the benefits of executive leadership are many—higher compensation, the potential for greater mobility, and the ability to influence across the entire organization, to name just a few. One of the big payoffs of being an executive comes down to the kind of impact you want to have, the influence you want to wield, and the way you want to spend your workdays. If you really want to make a difference by being in the driver's seat and determining the direction of the business, if you want to be at the core of possibility and make decisions that will set your business apart from the norm, and if you want to spend your days dealing with real issues and challenges so that you can be part of something bigger than you've ever imagined, then being an executive is worth the effort you'll put into it. The executive suite can be a very cool place to be if you are open to the possibilities.

Myth #6. I Will Have to Give Up My Personal Life to Be an Executive

I all too frequently hear from women that they just can't take on any more work—that their life is already too busy. I can't say that being an executive is any less busy a life than being a senior technical expert or a middle manager, but I can tell you that it's different and that, ultimately, you will have more control over your time when you are part of the senior leadership team. Let me explain: I think that middle management sometimes has the hardest job in the company, having to meet demands from so many different directions, and that life actually begins to get reasonable again when you become an executive—if you do it right. Being an executive involves less of actually "doing" the work and more of developing policy and strategy, orchestrating large-scale business initiatives, building high-performing teams, fostering supportive internal and external relationships, building collaborative coalitions, analyzing results to determine "midcourse corrections," and developing others to engage them and to leverage their talents.

As you can imagine, delegation is essential at the senior levels if you are going to be successful. I've also noticed that the best executives seem to find their own unique strategies for ensuring they have some sort of balance in their lives. For example, one of my colleagues is coaching an executive who has her assistant block off two hours on her calendar every day for her to get her own work done. During that time she has no meetings or calls. It's just quiet time to think, read, make decisions, answer e-mails, etc.—all those things that most of us try to do after we put the kids to bed at night.

As for balancing work with kids' activities, Betsy Lewis, a senior partner with Cooley Godward Kronish, often speaks to the women who attend SHAMBAUGH's Women in Leadership and Learning Program (WILL), and she gives this advice for achieving work-life balance: "Allow yourself to make a choice (between work and family) and then don't ever second-guess yourself." For example, her daughter was an avid soccer player throughout middle and high school. It often happened that Betsy had to choose between going to an important soccer match and attending a critical business meeting. While both were equally important to her, for very different reasons, she made a choice each time and then never allowed herself to second-guess her decision, realizing that her choice the next time might go the other way. At the executive level, you can make those kinds of decisions.

Another thing about life as an executive is that you can often set boundaries that support your family values. I work with a senior-level woman who found that when traveling for work, it was a problem to be away from home for long periods of time, and so she insisted that no travel within the United States could take her away from home for more than three consecutive days. Granted, she had more flights to deal with, but the benefit of feeling more "grounded" at home was worth it to her.

Finally, since executive positions often bring higher income, I know executives who have gained more time for their family, their gym workouts, and their outside interests by hiring housekeepers, personal chefs and trainers, lawn services, and even personal shoppers. The secret is to get the support systems in place that enable you to spend time where it's most important to you and then to make the situational choices that work best for you.

In summary, don't get caught up in the myths about being an executive. Look at the executives around you and be inspired rather than discouraged. Get the facts—ask your mentor or seek out a female executive, and you will likely find that these myths are nothing more than illusions. Of course, there will always be legitimate reasons why moving into the executive ranks might not be a good idea. Maybe it's not the right time for you, or maybe it's too risky (executives do get fired!), or maybe you just plain have to know too much. But if you carefully examine the truth and consider a promotion in the long-term view of your career and within the total context of your life, you might just decide that the rewards far outweigh the concerns. And then you'll be ready to move upward with enthusiasm.

Chapter Summary

- While there may legitimately be some obstacles that keep women from achieving their career goals, for the most part, women hold *themselves* back.
- Most women are stuck on a Sticky Floor of self-limiting assumptions, beliefs, and behaviors that prevent them from realizing their potential and moving to the next level of leadership. The Sticky Floors that hold women back from senior leadership positions are entirely different from those that prevent them from moving into midlevel management positions.
- In order to take a seat at the executive leadership table and create a truly Integrated Leadership team, women must assume responsibility for their own career advancement.
- The six most common false assumptions women have about senior leadership that prevent them from moving up are:
  - Executives are born leaders.
  - In order to get a promotion, I just need to do my job exceedingly well.
  - I have to be part of the "old boys' network" to be selected as an executive.

- ° Women are supportive and helpful advocates for other women.
- ° There are no real benefits to being an executive—just more hard work!
- ° I will have to give up my personal life to be an executive.

Chapter 11

Getting on the Right Escalator

ONE OF THE JOYS I have while writing a book is the opportunity to dialogue with sensational people. In an interview with Kathleen Matthews, executive vice president of Global Communications and Public Affairs at Marriott International, we talked about the tough but sometimes critical choices women have to make over the course of their career. Kathleen coined one of these decisions as "getting on the right escalator," which simply means moving in the right direction. She pointed out that it's all too easy to stay in your cubicle, head down, looking at your computer, rather than looking up and getting out. Kathleen is a perfect example of changing and getting on the right escalator when she left a very successful, 20-plus-year career as a news anchor and moved to the executive office of a Fortune 500 company.

I have to admit that I've been on the wrong escalator a few times in my corporate career. My personal challenges were positions where I was very comfortable with the daily tasks of the job and was well regarded for the results I produced. In those situations, I often missed other opportunities because I just wasn't interested; and frankly, those around me didn't encourage me to move on once I told them how much I liked what I was doing. There's something about maintaining the status quo that is very appealing in the short term. But I do remember feeling twinges when others would get a promotion or be chosen for a project that I felt I could have done better. Those were my clues that I needed to switch escalators!

The Steps of Getting on the Right Escalator

Step 1

The first step in getting on the right escalator is to know what direction you want to go. One of my favorite quotes is from *Alice in Wonderland* when the Cheshire cat tells Alice, "If you don't know where you're going, any road will get you there." The same is true for your career. If you don't have an idea of what's important to you, of how your career fits into your life goals, and of what real success looks like for you, how will you know which escalator is the right one for you at each stage of your career?

Kathleen Matthews also shared that, in her opinion, what's important in successfully navigating your career is to define your purpose (that is, what is important to you). It's easy to get caught up in the day-to-day crises and clutter and, without a purpose, lose sight of your course and full potential. To make the best career decisions, you need to ask yourself, "What do I want my life to look like?" And then, "How can I create that life for myself?" You have to invest in yourself—really get to know *you*, your values, core strengths, passions, and dreams.

Many of us are forced to look at this question of what is important to us when we're impacted by organizational changes such as mergers, acquisitions, or downsizings. But there are also other indicators that it might be time to move in another direction. Missing opportunities, not getting the recognition you deserve, and being in a demotivating environment that is draining your energy are all indications that you've stayed too long in one place or in a particular position and that it's time to reevaluate the direction of your career.

Step 2

The second step in getting on the right escalator is to consider your passions, interests, and special talents. All of these can help you legitimately decide the best direction for your career. I was a keynote speaker for a national women's sales leadership conference recently and met the number one saleswoman in the audience. Needless to say, she is amazing. When she introduced herself to me, I could tell immediately that she was in a good place—radiant, energized, and very successful. When I asked her how she came to be doing what she was doing, she told me that years ago her passion was helping people who were disadvantaged to secure financial stability and establish a sustainable lifestyle. She did financial planning with these individuals and helped literally hundreds of people to get their feet back on the ground. She later took this passion into the marketplace when she was asked to work with a financial planning organization where she now runs its global practice. She never in her wildest dreams thought her personal purpose and everlasting passion would evolve into this major sales leadership role.

In researching this book, I sat down with Steve Reinemund, prior chairman of the board of PepsiCo and now dean of business at Wake Forest University. He shared with me that he thinks there is too much emphasis on getting the highest-paying jobs, and consequently we are encouraging students to want the jobs with the greatest financial rewards, which are not always the best choices for them. He thinks it's more important to encourage students to pursue jobs based on what they love doing, in areas that they are passionate about and that give them the opportunity to build on their strengths. Steve's vision for today's graduates is a healthy perspective that is also essential for ensuring you are on a career path that brings meaning and purpose to your day-to-day life. This doesn't mean that there has to be a trade-off between making money and doing what you are passionate about. In fact, most of the successful executives I know are doing both! If you are both good at what you do and passionate about it, you are likely to be looking for the *up* escalator.

Step 3

The third and final step in getting on the right escalator is to bring to a conscious level those negative assumptions, fears, and concerns that fuel your internal voice that keeps giving you reasons why you should just stay right where you are, when your intuition is telling you that it might be time for a change.

To be successful and advance to greater levels of leadership, it's important that we as women get past our internal resistance, that voice in our head that says, "Not me" or "Not now." It's easy to let our negative assumptions and fears get in the way of taking on new opportunities that will get us out of the comfort zone. In particular women have a tendency to overanalyze the risks, which can be a limiting factor for advancement. When taking on a new role or stretch opportunity, I generally ask myself: What do I win and lose short and long term by taking this on? What are the benefits if I take this on and I do well? What do I have to lose if I take this on and it doesn't work out? What are some contingency plans if it doesn't work out?

I have found that once you break down the positives and negatives and you begin to understand what can actually go wrong, you begin to realize that most anything can be managed. And if things do go wrong, it's not the end of the world; in fact, in most cases we are better for it, based on the learning and growth that occurs. Tap into your support system and ask for advice—discuss your concerns with your supporters and gain their perspective. Finally, know that when people face change or a new challenge, they normally face some kind of fear—that's normal. By understanding that fear is normal, it can make it less intimidating and more in your control. I have found that taking on new challenges and experiences has offered the greatest opportunities for learning and growth, and, consequently, I've gained more confidence in myself. Then, when the next challenge comes along, I am more inclined and comfortable to tackle it head-on.

What Keeps Women from Finding the Right Escalator?

Having coached a number of women who feel that they have been held back in their career—either by an external factor such as limited opportunities within their company or by their own personal Sticky Floors—I know this is a simple question with a very complicated answer. So let me mention just a few factors that I see most often.

They Are Too Comfortable in the Comfort Zone

Women are often content to do a good job in their current position and sometimes need an external "nudge" to consider making a change. Mary Fontaine, an executive with Hay Group, shared with me that she thinks men are more aggressive about seeking broader opportunities much earlier in their career than women. Mary said, "I think women tend to stay in a particular job because they enjoy the mastery of the work until they are very confident and comfortable that they can do the job to a high standard of excellence, while men have a tendency to look for ways to move out of their comfort zone. This can create a problem for women, because if they stay too narrowly focused for too long, people never see them as a candidate for a bigger role."

This supports my research findings that managers, and even some mentors, see a woman as the subject-matter expert in a certain area. They then make the false assumption that she can't take on a broader role because while she might be technically brilliant, she is considered more tactical than strategic. For example, Sue may be known as an awesome director of research; however, she isn't thought of as a candidate for vice president of research and development because of the nontechnical requirements of that role.

They Tend to Not See Themselves as Executives

Hard as it is to imagine in today's business environment, some women still don't see themselves as executives. This is partially due to women being their own worst critic and partially due to their self-defeating assumptions, beliefs, and behaviors—the Sticky Floors. I recently sat down with my mentor and very dear friend Frances Hesselbein, president and CEO of the Frances Hesselbein Leadership Institute. She believes that while women have made progress, it's not enough. Part of the problem is the cultural obstacles to women's advancement that still exist. However, her greater concern is that very capable and smart women don't see themselves as CEOs or executives. Frances said, "All women need to do is *see themselves* as CEOs or executives, and the rest will follow. Of course, you have to work hard and prepare yourself, but women in some cases are already doing the job of an executive and just don't have the title."

SHAMBAUGH Leadership does many leadership 360-degree feedback assessments for women each year and then coaches them regarding their feedback. You wouldn't believe the number of women whose feedback providers describe them as having greater leadership abilities and potential than the women think they do. In fact, the first thing women generally look for in their feedback report is the areas that they are least strong in, potential development areas, or blind spots. To Frances's point, sometimes women don't acknowledge their potential, and, as a result, they don't dream big enough.

They Allow Others to Determine Their Career Path

Women are too often willing to let someone else decide which escalator they should ride. Let me give you a prime example. I was coaching a very smart and talented woman leader who felt stuck. She had been in her position for close to six years and felt good about the progress she had made with her team. She was hitting all her key objectives, and her team was well respected throughout the organization. Her boss was so pleased with her work, he said that when he left his position, she would be an excellent candidate as his replacement. She shared this with me with a sense of pride and comfort, thinking that her career advancement would be taken care of and that if she just kept doing a good job, she would automatically be promoted. (That was the first red flag!) Then she said that she and her boss had this very same conversation during her last three performance reviews, and so she assumed she was still on the right track. She never mentioned being concerned about the fact that she was still working for the same boss and leading the same team three years later. (That was the second red flag.)

This is just one situation that illustrates how women are not always as good as men at charting out their career and then actively managing their progress against specific career goals. Often, I find that a man will know what he wants his ultimate job to be. For example, I have a male colleague who knew that he wanted to be a CEO from the day he graduated from college. He was totally focused on that for a decade and only took positions that he thought would be a stepping-stone to the CEO level. It didn't matter to him what he did or where he did it as long as he could learn about a different part of the business and "punch his ticket" where he knew it mattered. And yes, he is a CEO now!

Some women get stuck because they don't think of the long-term goal or they are waiting to take their boss's job when he or she moves on. But did you know that in today's world, you have less than a 50:50 chance that will actually happen? With so many changes—mergers, acquisitions, reorganizations, and downsizings—no one can promise anything concrete these days. Stuff happens, and the best-laid plans don't always work out.

Don't let someone else figure out your career for you. And don't sit around waiting for your corporate Prince Charming to knock at your door. You can't expect someone else to take you to the top. It just doesn't happen that way. *You* have to manage *your* career.

They Are Reluctant to Get Off the *Wrong* Escalator

In my experience, women tend to feel embarrassed or guilty if a job is not working out. Well, this happens in many careers, and in some cases, it's worth working through the issues and giving it your best shot. But if you feel as though your position is not aligned with your goals and strengths, isn't taking you where you want to go, or isn't how you want to spend your days, then there's a good chance you are on the *wrong escalator*. It's all about being adaptable, flexible, and open to new opportunities in your career that is key to being successful in today's business environment.

I asked Pattie Sellers, editor at large and cochair, Most Powerful Women Summit at FORTUNE, what she has observed as important traits of the most successful women, and Pattie responded, "The women on the Fortune Most Powerful list embraced and I wholeheartedly believe you have to think of career not as a ladder but as a jungle gym. The world is changing so fast and unpredictably, we don't know what tomorrow's ideal job will be, which means you need to have sharp peripheral vision and look for opportunities all around. A lot of these women who have made the Fortune Most Powerful list have taken lateral moves in their careers, even some downward moves, to broaden their experience base and prepare them for bigger jobs. I think women are really good at being willing to do that because they don't care about rank and status as much as men do."

To Pattie's point, part of growing and being successful in your career is not always a linear path. It's important to keep your head up and be aware of changes happening in your organization and oppor-

tunities that occur. It's all about getting the right experience and exposure to set you up for greater leadership opportunities.

I think a lot of women say they don't mind staying in a role that
is not reflective of their goals or of who they really are, and yet deep
down they really do mind that they've had to compromise their aspirations. I have always believed that people who are not aligned with
their jobs—who don't feel purposefully connected with their work—
feel the impact on their energy level, their happiness, and, ultimately,
their overall effectiveness.

Tips for Getting—and Staying—on the Right Escalator

Here are some tips for taking stock of your career and determining if
it's time to jump on a different escalator to maximize your leadership
potential and move toward achieving your ultimate goals.

Recognize Your Greatness

Great leaders have the ability to look within themselves to understand
their beliefs, values, assumptions, goals, dreams, hopes, fears, strengths,
and weaknesses. It's all about knowing who you are and how to translate that into leadership capacity. Start seeing the greatness that you
have to offer as a leader. Start imagining yourself as a CEO, president,
executive director, and so on. If you can't see it, no one else will either.

Clarify What's Important to You

Another one of my favorite quotes comes from Oprah Winfrey: "You
can have it all. You just can't have it all at the same time." Along with
recognizing your greatness, another critical piece of self-discovery is

determining what's important to you at this particular stage in your life and where you want to be in three to five years. This is a conversation you usually have with significant others in your life. Do you really want to be an executive? Is now the right time for you?

It's also important for you to do your homework regarding the executive positions in your current organization. Take a serious look at what happens at the top—what values do you see demonstrated, and are they in sync with your own values? How do the executives behave? Are those the behaviors you want to live with on a daily basis? Can you see yourself working on that team?

In addition, ask yourself questions such as:

- *How much time and effort am I really willing to put into getting a promotion? How much am I willing to learn, do, and change to make it happen?*
- *Am I willing to ask for new opportunities and take the risks associated with doing something new that might be out of my comfort zone?*
- *Am I willing to talk with my boss about my current career path and my ultimate career goals?*
- *Am I willing to change organizations or even go to a new company (where my capabilities and strengths are recognized and my value is greater) as part of my overall career advancement strategy?*

Control Your Own Destiny

Don't wait for someone to hand you an instruction manual for your career. No one can map it out for you. You're going to have to figure it out for yourself and systematically lay the groundwork for your future. Map out a plan that takes into account both your situation and your aspirations. This is essential for getting on the right escalator at the right time!

Julie Daum, coleader of the North American Board & CEO Practice at Spencer Stuart, told me that she thinks what really determines the ability of people to advance to the senior ranks is the kinds of positions they choose along the way. She said, "If you want to run an organization, you need to have line experience. If you are interested in advancing to more of a senior generalist position, you need to broaden your business acumen and expand your experience; so take on nonstaff roles, move out of marketing into sales, or take on those visible positions that are tied to bottom-line business results. It's also key to recognize that sometimes you need to ask for a position like a line job or an international assignment."

It's also important to know that when it comes to the direction of your career, there is no right or wrong. It's about knowing yourself and becoming aware of any potential misalignment. Then you ask yourself, *What steps do I take now to change this situation?*

Once you have a plan, take stock of your strengths, consider where your organization is going, and then proactively move in a direction where you can add value to the business while staying true to your values, goals, and commitments. Here are a few ideas:

- Consider hiring a coach for a short amount of time to help you put a career plan together and to stay committed to that process.
- Begin to strategically and intentionally create specific experiences for yourself that will close gaps in your skill set or give you greater visibility.
- Schedule lunch with or reach out to someone who can give you good advice, someone who can share a unique perspective, or someone who should know about you (a potential supporter or connector).
- Go back to school and take a course that will help you build your qualifications for opportunities that interest you.

- Join an organization that will bring you into contact with others in your industry and concentrate on building a broader external network.

By taking steps like these, you will control your own future and won't have to rely on someone else to pull you forward.

Don't Assume Others Know Your Career Goals

Unless you are very lucky and have a coach or mentor who has taken the time to learn about your career aspirations, chances are that people assume you are happy doing what you are currently doing without considering where you might like to be in the future or even what you might want to be doing differently now. So it's very important to communicate your career goals with people who are aware of and connected to potential opportunities. You also need to make your work results, specific accomplishments, unique skills, and particular interests known to others throughout your organization.

It's essential to get people on board who recognize your value and know your ultimate career goals, so that when opportunities arise, they are there to champion and support you. If you don't, those around you (with all good intentions) may put you in a box that isn't where you really want to be. Julie Daum pointed out, "You need to make people aware of what you want so that when they are considering candidates for various positions, they know what's in your head. And if it's not what they think you should be doing, then you can at least have a legitimate conversation about it."

Get Feedback from Others

Feedback is invaluable. The more you know about yourself, the more confident and resilient you will be. But getting feedback is not always easy, and women tend to take constructive but difficult feedback personally. Katharine Frase, vice president of Industries Research at IBM, said, "I think the hardest thing for us to hear is how we come across versus how we intend to come across. For a long time I was the youngest person in the room. And then came some magical day when I was no longer the youngest person in the room, but I didn't realize it. I remember my manager taking me aside one day and telling me I gave a fine presentation but it was time to drop the 'cute.' I was first offended, as 'cute' wasn't what I was going for at all. However, I realized that I was still carrying with me mannerisms that may have worked at 25 but didn't work at 40."

Katharine's example is one that I share with many leaders when it comes to getting feedback. Rather than being defensive, we must be open-minded, consider the feedback a gift, and take it seriously. Like Katharine, if you take this approach, you will learn things about yourself that you can't see—your blind spots. You will also gain more respect from and credibility with others.

One of the best ways to determine how we are showing up as a leader is to do a 360-degree feedback assessment process. Many organizations have these available for their managers. If your organization doesn't, there are excellent 360-degree assessments available commercially. I encourage every leader who hasn't done a leadership 360-degree feedback assessment to do one right away and get a coach to help interpret the results. You will discover that your blind spots will be as much in your areas of strength as in your opportunities for improvement. Some questions to consider when reviewing your feedback include What is your leadership style? Where are you most effective? What are your blind spots? How might you be more effective as a leader? And what do others see as your key strengths and unique value proposition? With this very valuable feedback, you can dramatically alter your self-talk and reach for greater levels of leadership.

Self-awareness also means gaining *informal* feedback on how others view us regarding our leadership potential and our reputation. Reach out to others to ask their advice and feedback regarding your effectiveness as a leader. Look for people who can be a good source of credible feedback for you, and then be sure to leverage those opportunities to gain new and valuable insights.

In all of SHAMBAUGH's Women in Leadership and Learning courses, we start off with the notion that our leadership is a reflection of the perceptions that others have of us. That's why it is so critical to discern what we want that perception of our leadership to be and then to look at ways to *be* it consistently. Some questions to consider when seeking informal feedback on this are:

- **How are you doing?** How are you perceived by others as compared with your peers? Who knows about you, and who should know who you are and what you can do . . . but probably doesn't? Do you have your personal "board of directors" who can tell you how well you're doing and what folks are saying about you as a leader?
- **What results are you getting?** How are you measuring your effectiveness? How is your team doing, and how is it measuring its success? Who knows about those results, and how do they add value to their part of the business? When you have success, do the right people know about it?
- **What are your strengths and weaknesses?** What do others think you do well (what are you "famous" for?), and where do they think you could do better or know more, etc.
- **What are your blind spots?** What can others share about you that you don't already know?
- **What are your key differentiators?** What is your *unique* value proposition? Why might you be chosen for a senior position over your potential competition?

Find the Courage to Get Out of Your Comfort Zone

When I interviewed Pattie Sellers, I asked her what was her favorite piece of advice at the 2011 Fortune Most Powerful Summit. Pattie said it was from Ginni Rometty, and this was just a few weeks before Ginni was named the new CEO of IBM. Pattie reported that Ginni said that growth and comfort do not coexist and that every time she's grown as a person and as an executive, it's been a really uncomfortable situation, so push yourself constantly beyond your comfort levels. To Ginni Rometty's point, some of your greatest growth and most significant breakthroughs will come as a result of taking a risk. Karen Bechtel, managing director of the Carlyle Group, shared with me, "If you are interested in growing, learning, and advancing in your career, it's important that you get outside of your comfort zone. If you just get out there and do it, you will learn what works and what doesn't. I've done a lot of cold calling in my life and sometimes it worked, sometimes it didn't, but you pick yourself up and go again."

A common denominator of all the successful executives and leaders I have met is that they have had the courage to take on opportunities or new jobs that required them to get out of their comfort zone. It may not have come easy the first time, but after doing it a few times, it didn't seem as difficult. An important aspect that determines our willingness to move beyond our comfort zone is our mindset—it's how we view and approach a situation. Here are a few questions that will help you evaluate your own mindset around this important aspect of leadership:

- How often do you get out of your comfort zone and take a risk?
- When was the last time you volunteered to do something totally different from your normal job?
- Do you take on new roles or engage with different teams?
- How often do you volunteer to help out on other projects?

- Is your team looking for new and challenging opportunities?
- Is your team volunteering to do work that is new and different from its current responsibilities?

Many times what holds us back from taking risks is that voice in our head that tries to convince us to not step out. However, the more steps you take outside your comfort zone, the more confident and competent you will become. Over time it will become more comfortable and natural to take on new roles you might not have considered before, to explore stretch opportunities, to reach out to someone you don't know, to walk into a room and take control, or to share your ideas. Here are a few pieces of advice for taking those first steps:

- I've found that it's easier to take risks when you are truly committed or passionate about something.
- It helps to reach out and ask others for advice—those who have the experience and insights that will truly make a difference for you.
- Be wise and prudent about the risks you choose to take, map out the potential obstacles, consider the worst-case scenarios, and then develop contingency plans as you go along.

When you do step out of your comfort zone, look back on the experience and ask yourself: *What did I learn from this? What did I do well, and what would I do differently?* And finally, don't be discouraged if you make a few mistakes. It doesn't matter if you're wildly successful or disappointed with your results, because the experience itself will be the learning journey. Great leaders learn as much from their failures as they do from their successes.

Decide what you want out of your career, map out a plan to get there, and then put yourself in a position to achieve it. If you think it's time to get on the up escalator, then read on, as I'm going to tell you just what to do!

Chapter Summary

- "Getting on the right escalator" means moving in the right direction.
- There are three key steps for getting on the right escalator:
  1. Know what direction you want to go.
  2. Consider your passions, interests, and special talents.
  3. Bring to a conscious level the negative assumptions and fears that keep you from moving on when your intuition is telling you it's time for a change.
- Here are more tips for maximizing your leadership potential and achieving your ultimate goals:
  - Recognize your greatness and see yourself as an executive.
  - Clarify what's important to you.
  - Control your own destiny and career path.
  - Don't assume others know your career goals.
  - Get feedback from others about your strengths and weaknesses, blind spots, and key differentiators.
  - Find the courage to get out of your comfort zone.
  - Don't be afraid to get off the *wrong* escalator (i.e., change course if you're headed in the wrong direction).

Chapter 12

Leverage Your Personal Power

Now that you know what it takes to get your career moving in the right direction, let's look at one of the most critical things you can do to "show up" as being ready to move into a senior leadership role. Showing up as a powerful person is key for success at all levels, but it is essential for moving into a senior position and for operating successfully once you get there.

When we teach our Power and Influence leadership programs, we define power as "the ability to effect change or the right others give you to influence them." In other words, power leads to possibility! I believe that anyone in an organization can have power, regardless of their title, and use it to positively affect key results and decisions that pertain to their area of responsibility. Some people can even use their power to impact decisions on a broader level and influence large-scale change initiatives. Leaders who have power are able to inspire and motivate others, change people's thinking, create shifts in the corporate culture, and influence social trends by harnessing people's hearts and minds. The more power you have, the more capacity you have to make a difference for those that you serve as well as for the causes that you care about.

One of the most crucial differences between men and women in leadership is the way in which and the extent to which they use their power. Men are much more likely than women to recognize and leverage their power within the organization. For example, men feel as though their power gives them the right to make decisions and tell people what to do, while women generally try to gain agreement. Women often don't recognize when people want someone to make a decision—any decision—rather than spend time talking about it.

Many women have misconceptions about power. Some think that power is solely connected to a position or title and that it doesn't apply to them in their current job. In fact, based on a study ("Women and the Paradox of Power"), 41 percent of women feel they don't have enough power to perform effectively in their present job. Some women even think that *power* is a bad word! I've heard from a number of women that having power seems manipulative or self-serving.

Not understanding power, what it is or how to leverage it, prevents many women from trying to have influence in certain situations and even stops them from attempting to be heard. This single factor can hold them back from competing for promotional opportunities.

Linda Rabbitt, chairman and CEO of Rand Construction Corporation and a member of several boards, including the Board of the Federal Reserve Bank of Richmond, said to me in an interview that the idea of power as good or bad "all depends on what your motivation is. My motivation wasn't to be powerful or rich. My motivation starting out was a need to survive. But eventually it was fun to be impactful. It was fun to make a difference, to feel that your being in the room changed the course of events." To Linda's point, having power can have a positive impact on those around you. It's a beautiful thing when you realize not only that you have power, but that you can use it to make this world a better place.

Gail Evans, a colleague of mine who is a speaker and author on women-in-leadership issues, told me, "Women won't realize their power until they believe that they have it and that they truly belong in powerful positions. Once that happens, they will use it very effectively. Unfortunately, we aren't there yet because women are wired to downplay the power they have and don't know how to increase their power base."

The bottom line is, if you don't know you have power, you can't use it. So let's look at women's sources of power and ways to better leverage them. There are several foundational elements of power, and they fall into two categories: Personal Power and Organizational Power. Most women focus on Organizational Power—that is, the power we get from our position or role in the organization. We will talk about Organizational Power in the next chapter. But Personal Power is just as valuable as Organizational Power. So let's start with that.

Be Authentic

One of the overarching themes of Personal Power is being authentic. Authenticity means consistently being your true self *and* being true *to* yourself. I once read that we spend the first half of our lives being the person others want us to be and the second half being who we really are! I suggest that you be who you really are, right now. Being authentic means acknowledging and embracing who you are and then using that insight as your internal navigation system. This, in and of itself, is very powerful!

Authenticity comes from self-awareness. Leveraging your Personal Power is predicated on knowing yourself honestly and deeply. Each of us at times operates on an unconscious level, and we don't recognize our true values and strengths, or what I refer to as our *Sticky Floors*—those beliefs, assumptions, and behaviors that can limit our ability to reach the next level of leadership. If you want to increase your Personal Power, you need to take a long, hard, honest look at yourself. I encourage you to refer to my book *It's Not a Glass Ceiling, It's a Sticky Floor*, which focuses on the importance of self-awareness.

The key to being an authentic leader is to be crystal clear about your core values, beliefs, and principles and then always act in alignment with them. As other people recognize this consistency, their trust and respect for you will grow. As a result, your influence and Personal Power will also grow.

Here are some additional ways you can increase your self-awareness and authenticity:

- **Accept who you are as a leader.** Identify your leadership values and principles and share them in a meaningful way with others in your organization. Recognize your core leadership styles and learn to be flexible, given the situation, but consistent in your general approach.
- **Express your true self and tell your own story.** Find the right time and place to share a piece of who you are by reflecting your genuine feelings about yourself or a situation. Share what you have learned, cared about, and stand for in a way that helps others feel "connected" to you.

The Sources of Personal Power

Your Personal Power comes from four sources:

1. Knowledge

Sir Francis Bacon said, "Knowledge is power," and it's true! This is one of the most important sources of power for executives. Knowledge refers not only to the things you know, but also to your skills and abilities as well as your accomplishments. Your knowledge base is why people come to you for advice or assistance, trust what you say, and even invite you to critical meetings. The more knowledge you have, the more helpful and valuable you are to others.

The good news is that knowledge is available to virtually everyone with the desire to pursue it! Linda Rabbitt, mentioned earlier, shared with me, "Successful people are really interested in the world and how it works. They're thirsty for knowledge; they really want to understand whatever it is they have an interest in."

The secret to leveraging your knowledge is realizing that it only gives you power when others recognize and value what you know and when it differentiates you from others—in other words, when people respect you for your "thought leadership."

Here are some strategies to leverage your knowledge:

- **Translate your knowledge into value for others.** To gain power, it's not enough to know something; you have to be able to apply that knowledge in ways that others value. For example, in the book *The 11 Secrets of Highly Influential IT Leaders*, Marc Schiller explains that IT executives leverage their knowledge in terms of their *credibility*. Clients don't really care how much IT executives know. They want to be able to believe what IT is telling them and be assured that IT will be able to do what it promises! I think we can all learn a lesson from this. To leverage your knowledge, learn to apply it in valuable and visible ways and work to increase your credibility both inside and outside your organization.
- **Focus as much on expanding your knowledge as you do on delivering results.** Create your own list of "best practices" and "lessons learned" after a major project has been completed. Commit to learning something new every day. Every Friday, ask yourself, *What have I learned this week that can make me a better leader?* Encourage your team to embrace continual improvement and look for ways to improve current processes and procedures.

- **Think beyond your technical or functional knowledge.**
  Whatever technical or functional expertise you bring to your
  organization, realize that executives also need strong business
  acumen. At the higher levels of an organization, a solid
  combination of technical smarts and business savvy is
  essential. Be sure you are broadening your overall business
  insights and experience.
- **Consider your contribution ahead of time.** In most business
  situations, it's important that you bring something to the
  table—whether it's your technical expertise, thought
  leadership, or creative ideas. So be prepared. Before an
  important meeting, think about how you can bring value to
  a particular item on the agenda.
- **Continually increase your knowledge base.** Don't let your
  knowledge and experience get stale or out of date. Take
  different assignments that will stretch your thinking in

creative ways, get involved in internal and external committees, or explore the resources and activities of industry groups. You might even offer to take different activities off your manager's plate in order to gain broader experience and visibility. Continual learning is your competitive advantage.

2. Leadership Persona

Successful executives have something unique about them that has nothing to do with their technical competence or skills. It's more about how they affect us through their physical presence, demeanor, presentation of thoughts, and general mode of interaction. My definition of leadership persona is "having the ability to connect authentically with the thoughts and feelings of others in order to motivate and inspire them." To put it in real terms, think of a situation when someone walks into the room and immediately gets everyone's attention. When the person speaks, everyone listens. When that person leaves, people want to go along. That's leadership persona!

If people were to describe your leadership persona, what would they say about you? Are you approachable? How do people feel around you? Your persona helps you to stand out from others. Some call it "executive presence." It's that "wow" factor that you create because of who you are. In many cases, it's what people remember best about you. The greater your attraction, the greater your power.

Karen Bechtel, managing director of the Carlyle Group, has worked for years in a predominantly male industry, and yet she has created her own presence and persona, which is known by many on Wall Street. Karen shared with me that she tries to inject her personality into every meeting or conversation, and as a result people remember her. Karen said, "It's important to remember that people 'take away' impressions about the people they engage with. Therefore I always leave something of myself in a discussion."

SHAMBAUGH interviewed over 80 women executives to identify the following characteristics that you can use as a road map for creating your own leadership persona:

- **Candor.** Being honest through your willingness to constructively "tell it like it is"
- **Clarity.** Communicating your ideas in an intuitively clear and compelling way
- **Openness.** Not prejudging and being willing to consider another point of view
- **Passion.** Expressing your commitment, motivation, and drive in a way that shows people you really believe in something
- **Poise.** Appearing sophisticated and conveying a solid background of education as well as experience
- **Self-confidence.** Being sure of yourself, such that others know you have the required strength and resolve
- **Sincerity.** Believing in and meaning what you say
- **Thoughtfulness.** Thinking through something before responding
- **Warmth.** Being accessible to others and interested in them

3. Resilience

I realize that resilience hasn't always been considered a source of power. In fact, it's only become a hot topic since the economy put so many businesses and individuals in difficult situations. But now it's recognized, by executives and corporate boards, as a key requirement of successful leaders. My definition of resilience is "the capacity to bounce back from misfortune, disruptive change, and failures." Resiliency is driven by our intrinsic qualities (attitudes and behaviors) that keep us from giving up, allow us to muster the strength to face challenges, and ultimately enable us to stay on course to reach our goals.

While we all have setbacks and disappointments, those who are resilient—who can bounce back from adversity and become even stronger as a result—are powerful people. They are out front in the face of challenge and embrace difficult situations. They consistently use their creative and positive mindset to power through and come out better in the end.

Here are some strategies to build your resilience:

- **Have a positive mindset.** See the glass as half full rather than half empty! No one wants to work with or for someone who is habitually negative.
- **Embrace change.** Change isn't always comfortable, but if you realize that change brings opportunities, you can welcome it and revel in the possibilities. Those who help to interpret, enhance, and implement change are seen as strong leaders because leadership is essentially all about change.
- **Manage your energy.** How are you managing your energy now? Identify what gives you energy and try to eliminate any nonessential activities that drain your energy. Know when your energy is high and leverage those times to address the most important issues, have the toughest conversations, and make your strongest impressions.
- **Manage your reactions.** Control your immediate response to people and situations and give yourself a choice in terms of how you react. In difficult situations, make a plan to be proactive and don't allow your emotions to rule your thinking.
- **Move your purpose forward and keep it alive.** Get clear about what you want for yourself and your team. Become focused and intentional in everything you do to make the *most important* things happen. Learn ways to keep yourself and others on track in spite of everything else that creeps into the picture.

- **Be courageous and never give up.** Get "unstuck" by standing up for something you believe in, confronting traditional ways of thinking, or doing something that is definitely out of your comfort zone. Leverage your sheer determination and rigorous persistence to achieve your goals and exceed your wildest expectations!
- **Remember to laugh.** Use humor. It can stimulate creativity and help get people engaged and energized. People like to be around others who can poke fun at themselves. In the scheme of things, we can't sweat the small stuff.

4. Communication

Your ability to effectively communicate, both verbally and in writing, is key to gaining the respect and credibility you need to be an effective executive. How others perceive you often depends on how you present your ideas, opinions, and arguments. While many factors, such as style, timing, and tone, are important in communication, the areas where women can gain the greatest leverage deal with focus, inspiration, and argument. Women differentiate themselves, and impress others, by staying on point and being succinct, motivating others, and being able to hold their own in a debate.

Our personal expressiveness often establishes our level of credibility, affects our ability to influence decisions, and ultimately determines whether or not we are invited to join the inner circle—which is the key to the executive suite. Of all our sources of power, this one might be the most important for you to think about because it leaves a lasting impression. Here are some strategies to leverage your communication:

- **Be clear and succinct.** My father once told me, "It's better to speak little and say much than to speak much and say little!" Essentially he was telling me to be a woman of few words and to stay on point. Sometimes "less is more" in order to exude confidence and authority as well as to get people to listen to you. Women often communicate by giving lots of details, talking about how we *feel* about a situation, and trying to involve everyone in the conversation. This doesn't always produce the results we want as effectively as being more direct and succinct. People are busy, and they are constantly inundated with information. My advice is be a women of a few words. Provide context, facts, and rationale in your messages (even quantify things—percentages can be powerful), but be sure you are substantive, concise, and correct!

- **Always own your message.** When you have something important to say, you have to speak up. This opportunity may come up when you are in meetings, when you need to deliver tough feedback, or when you don't agree with a particular direction in which something is headed. This also means owning your own words and not assigning blame to someone else—also known as playing the blame game. People respect others who speak the truth, who don't sugarcoat the issues. However, it is *how* you speak up that determines if people will listen to you and take you seriously. Act confident, balance emotion with logic, present relevant facts and information, and time your contribution so it's relevant to the conversation. You don't want others to *interpret* your view; you want them to clearly understand your intention, position, and perspective.

- **Be inspiring.** To be powerful, your thoughts must be relevant to others and move them emotionally as well as intellectually. You accomplish this by enthusiastically and convincingly appealing to someone's values, emotions, or feelings. Being impressive, motivational, or inspirational can stimulate people to do extraordinary things. The power of inspiration comes from connecting with people's hearts. Share stories to illustrate your vision and values. Use images and metaphors to paint a picture that is exciting and captivates people when they see themselves in it. Don't be afraid to show your authentic enthusiasm, commitment, dedication, or passion in order to amplify your voice.

- **Learn how to present arguments well.** As an executive, you're going to have to be able to "stick your neck out" once in a while. There will be times when you'll need to let people know where you stand on an issue, even if others don't agree with you. This is what we call *having conviction*. It's important to be able to effectively disagree with someone's view, challenge someone's assumption, actively affirm your view, and actually engage in a debate. This can feel like conflict for some women, which is a problem for those who prefer to avoid confrontation. Of course, there is a right time and way to do this. For free tips on how to effectively present your side of an issue, go to http://www.shambaughleadership.com.

Personal Power is within our control. It's all about who we are, what we know, and how we act. Now is the time to start thinking about what kind of power you have, what kind of power you want, and how you can build your power base.

Chapter Summary

- Leaders who have power are able to inspire and motivate others, change people's thinking, and create shifts in the corporate culture.
- *Many women have misconceptions about power and therefore are less likely* than men to recognize and leverage their power.

- The foundational elements of power fall into two categories: Personal and Organizational.
- Personal Power comes from four sources:
  1. **Knowledge.** Not only the things you know, but also your skills, abilities, and accomplishments
  2. **Leadership persona.** The ability to connect authentically with the thoughts and feelings of others in order to motivate and inspire them
  3. **Resiliency.** The capacity to bounce back from misfortune, disruptive change, and failures
  4. **Communication.** The ability to effectively communicate
- The key to Personal Power is being authentic—consistently being your true self and being true to yourself.

Chapter 13

Leverage Your Organizational Power

As THE TERM SUGGESTS, your Organizational Power is somewhat dependent on your role in the organization. But like Personal Power, it also relates to who you are and what you do in regard to your reputation and your network.

The Four Key Areas of Organizational Power

1. Role

This pertains directly to your position or title in the organization. Classic hierarchical power, important in command-and-control organizations, comes into play here. People usually respect the authority of your position, especially when you are a manager. When you are in this position, you will have control of rewards (such as job assignments) and punishments (such as negative performance reviews), which means that people will give you the right to tell them what to do and how to do it. They will also listen to you and determine when you are making suggestions versus when you are being directive. The higher you are in an organization, the more power you will assume from this source.

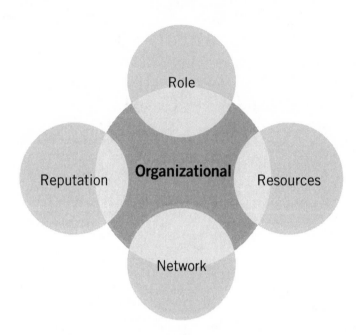

With all that said, you don't have to wait for a new position to enhance your role in the organization. Instead, you can increase your power in the role you already have. Here are some tips for how to do this:

- **Seek work that has more impact.** Look for opportunities to work on mission-critical projects that will impact key business objectives and contribute to the organization in ways that will provide greater exposure and visibility for you and your team.
- **Think outside the box.** Join committees that make key decisions and get involved in task forces that directly impact the bottom line of the business and will give you a broader knowledge of business acumen.
- **Continue to look at ways to reinvent yourself and your team.** It's important that you watch the trends in your company and make sure your role is not being devalued. When

coaching leaders in this area, I encourage them to conduct what I refer to as informational interviews. This requires them to identify several people both inside and outside their functional area who will be honest and provide a helpful, often different perspective. This is a great way to learn more about the direction of the company, where the potential opportunities are being created and where you can best align yourself. The knowledge you gain through these interviews may call for you to reinvent your job or team by rethinking your value proposition, expanding your skills sets, and seeking new ways you can be of value to other functional areas across the enterprise.

- **Recognize your value.** Identify exactly what you have to offer. Consider information and insights you might share or people you know who might be able to help someone out. And when you are talking with others, don't hesitate to ask them about the challenges they are facing so that you can be thinking about how you can help them.

2. Resources

If you control resources that others in the organization want or need, the simple allocation of these resources can give you power. In addition, the quantity (or even quality) of the people that work for you can impact this source of power indirectly. Having a strong team can be very valuable to you, particularly when everything tightens up in the industry. Ideally, you can differentiate you and your team by leveraging your unique value proposition and being recognized for your diversity of thought and results-oriented attitude, all of which are valued by your customers and colleagues.

Having a strong and diverse team that works well together is the key for enhancing your power base in terms of applying and allocating this key resource. Here are some tips for building up your people resources:

- **Develop your team.** Beth J. Green, corporate manager of Supply Chain RSKOM & Strategy at Northrop Grumman, shared with me, "It's important to develop your informal team in a multitude of areas because your value to others may involve a whole array of knowledge, experience, and skills for which your formal team may not currently be best in class."
- **Be forward thinking.** Get out of your office and speak with senior executives. Attend cross-functional strategy sessions to learn more about the challenges and growth areas of your company. Then, based on that information, determine new and innovative ways your team can have a visible impact on the business or provide a substantial "win" for someone on the executive team.
- **Let others know what you and your team can do for them.** You only have power from a particular source if others know about it! If you and your team are doing great things but others in the organization don't know about them, you don't have that particular resource as a source of power.

Remember, you and your team's unique value proposition helps to differentiate you from others and enhance your thought leadership. However, executives are busy, and so you have to identify natural ways to ensure they know what you and your team have accomplished and how that connects to key business goals and objectives.

3. Network

While your position may give you a certain amount of power, you can always gain more through affiliation with other people. Likewise, your competence and overall performance are important, but your relationships and social capacity are equally important. If you know the CEO or have the ear of other influential people and executives, people will pay more attention to what you think and say. The breadth and depth of the contacts you have can provide a perception of your power . . . the more people you know, the more they can help you influence others.

Your relationships should cover a broad spectrum of people to include colleagues, customers, mentors, sponsors, key influencers, and subject-matter experts—to name just a few. The broader and more diverse your network, the greater knowledge, insight, and strategic perspective you will have. An established network also helps you address complex issues, build strategic alliances, and spread the word about your team's value proposition. Here are some tips for expanding your network:

- **Be open to and curious about everyone you meet.** Always be on the lookout for people with whom you might want to establish a connection and whom you might want to introduce to someone else. Consider every business meeting and social function as a networking opportunity. Be sure to get (and give) business cards!
- **Make a plan to reach out to others and then do it.** Some leaders actually set a goal for meeting or reconnecting with a certain number of people each month. They see this as critical to their success and treat it as they do their other work-related action items. They recognize that it's mission critical to know others and be known!
- **Build strategic alliances.** Create networks of supporters who share the value of your proposition. Consider building win-win relationships with individuals throughout your organization and within your customer base as well as in

your industry. Attend business functions for the sheer purpose of making new connections that are a part of your networking plan. The law of reciprocity works well in these situations. When you meet new people, think about how you might be of value to them. If you help them, they will likely help you in return.

- **Create your own personal "board of directors."** This concept is so important in almost every facet of our careers that I discussed it also in Chapter 11. If you have read my previous book, *It's Not a Glass Ceiling, It's a Sticky Floor*, you'll remember that I devoted several pages there to this idea as well. Essentially what I mean by this is to engage a carefully selected group of individuals in your decision making and action planning. This is especially helpful when you are thinking of making a move in your career. Their perspective and insights can be invaluable.

- **Think broad and big.** Include people in your network who have knowledge about what's going on both inside and outside your organization and who are both well respected and influential. Remember, if you align yourself with power brokers, you will also have power (by association); so be politically savvy and build meaningful relationships with these people.

- **Learn from others—continually.** Be sure you have many coaches, mentors, and sponsors throughout your career. Engage with a broad spectrum of people you can learn from—whether they are customers, colleagues, direct reports, marketplace experts, or even community leaders. Embrace the pure intention of learning from all the people you meet or currently know. Pick their brains and test your assumptions with them. Remember that knowledge is power and insight is even greater power!

- **Bring something to the table.** As you reach out to others, it's important that you bring something to the table—whether it's your technical expertise, thought leadership, ideas on a burning issue, or a new opportunity that would help the business. For example, before an important meeting, try to put yourself in the leader's shoes and think about how you might bring value to something that is important to him or her. Become known for being able to solve problems and offer innovative solutions on a professional as well as a personal level.

4. Reputation

Recent research, as well as the work by Steven Covey, indicates that this is a very valuable source of power for you. The two most essential elements of your reputation are trust and credibility. Trust is an important component of turning your power into influence, and trust is based on predictability. When people know that you are authentic and true to yourself, they will be more likely to want to agree with and support you because they will trust that you mean what you say. Likewise, when people know that you are honest and have a keen sense of integrity and if they believe that you know what you are talking about—in other words, if you are credible—they are more likely to listen to you and want to do as you recommend.

Building your reputation involves "walking your talk"—making sure that your actions are always consistent with your words. When you act in alignment with your core values, beliefs, and principles, you will become known as a trustworthy and credible leader. Identify your internal drivers and align your words and actions so that they demonstrate and support what is most important to you. Do what you say you are going to do, because actions really do speak louder than words.

Related to reputation is the concept of a personal brand. While reputation is usually seen as the by-product of your actions and behaviors, a personal brand is described as the "conversations people have about you." Your personal brand must be developed with rigor and intention—much like companies build the brand for their products in order to make them more marketable. Can you see the connection? You want control of what people think and say about you in order to ensure that you are recognized for your unique strengths, get credit for your accomplishments, and are viewed as executive material. What are you *known* for? Do you have the *respect* of your peers? Does senior management know about your *accomplishments*?

Your personal brand is something that you need to continue to build, reinforce, and socialize throughout your career, but it is especially essential when you are hoping to enter the executive suite. Decide what you want your reputation to be and then create the perception you want others to have of your signature strengths and unique leadership talent.

So how do you go about building your personal brand? Here are the key steps:

- Write down eight words or phrases that you would like people to use to describe you. Be sure to include what you know that makes you highly promotable into the executive ranks, such as "strategic" and "innovative."
- For each word or phrase, identify exactly what you might say or do to show up this way. Think of people you know who are described this way and consider what they do or say that creates that impression of them. Write down at least three actions for each word or phrase.
- Conduct a reality check by asking a few people whom you really trust to write down 8 to 10 words or phrases that they think describe you. Compare those lists with your list and

identify the areas where you need to create or change a particular impression.

- Think about situations at work where you can demonstrate that you are, in fact, the way you want to be described. Proactively plan for that in at least two situations each week. Then check with someone you trust and respect to give you honest feedback about how you were actually perceived in those particular situations.

- Finally, think about the individuals who are most crucial to your advancement. Those are the people you want to make sure are aware of your personal brand. Consider how you can proactively make that happen. This is when having an internal sponsor in the executive ranks can be very helpful.

- Create a strong brand for your team using the same process. Remember, your team represents you throughout the organization. You want your team to be known and recognized for the value it brings to the organization.

There is one more thing I want to mention about power. It has a very special aspect that few people realize: it grows exponentially!

I sat down with Candy Duncan, managing partner at KPMG, and she shared this thought with me: "Power is not always what you have within yourself. In fact, you can access a greater power base by empowering others." In other words, the more power you give away to others, the easier it is for you to ultimately influence more people and therefore grow your own power. Candy told me that when she builds a team, she strives for diversity in order to get a variety of perspectives and the greatest potential strengths. She then looks for ways to give away her power by pushing decision making down and putting her team in charge. Candy said that this strategy has resulted in a greater competitive advantage by leveraging the whole team's power rather than just her own. In fact, clients tell her that they value the thought leadership that they can draw from her team rather than from just one person.

So don't be afraid to give away your power—you don't have to hold onto it all the time. Not only does shifting power this way give your team the opportunity to learn and grow, but it also increases your power base and credibility in the long run.

Thoughts to Consider About Personal and Organizational Power

Now that you have learned more about your Personal and Organizational Power, I invite you to think about a few things:

- Do you currently have the power necessary to be effective in your existing role?
- Which of the eight dimensions (four Personal Power, four Organizational Power) are currently your greatest sources of power?
- Which one of these sources of power presents the greatest challenge for you, and how can you begin to strengthen that particular area?
- How can you access a greater power base to advance your leadership?
- How can you use these sources of power to effect change or influence something across the broader spectrum of your organization?

Remember, executives who have power are able to get things done. They are better able to motivate, inspire, and influence others when they need a greater level of cooperation or when they are trying to facilitate a difficult change in their organization. The more power you have, the better you are positioned for advancing to the executive levels. So if you have power, please consider it an asset and use it!

Chapter Summary

Organizational Power comes from four sources:

1. **Role, position, title.** Enhance your power by recognizing your value and continually reinventing yourself.

2. **Control and allocation of resources (specifically the human resource of people).** Enhance your power by developing your team and finding innovative ways the team can have a visible impact on the business.

3. **Breadth and depth of your network.** Develop a plan to intentionally and purposefully expand your network through affiliations and strategic alliances.

4. **Reputation.** The two most essential elements of reputation are trust and credibility; enhance your power by developing your personal brand.

Chapter 14

Showing Up Strategic

WHILE LEVERAGING THEIR POWER is perhaps the single most important thing women can do to improve their chances of advancing into the senior ranks, showing up strategic is also extremely important. When I work with SHAMBAUGH's clients and I see talented women who have been on the cusp of advancing to the executive suite for years and yet still aren't there, I often bring up the subject with the organization's top leaders. One of the most common reasons I hear for women's lack of advancement is that they are not strategic enough. While I understand that many women may not have had P&L roles or line positions, I truly think women are very strategic thinkers.

My experience coaching hundreds of women, as well as SHAMBAUGH's research and body of work, tells me that women are in fact strategic. Let's face it; women have been juggling multiple roles, at work and home, for decades now, and this has required us to hone a myriad of critical problem-solving skills that are totally related to strategic thinking. So it's not that we aren't strategic; it's that we aren't showing up that way. Showing up as strategic rather than tactical involves others' perceptions, and when it comes to promotions, perceptions *are* reality!

Wherever we are in our lives, we need to ask ourselves how we can be strategic in getting what we want. We must take responsibility for getting a sponsor, for understanding the environment in which we work, for determining whom we need to build relationships with, and for getting our ideas across. Betsy Myers, leadership expert, author of *Take the Lead*, and founding director of the Center for Women and Business at Bentley University, said that she tells women, "Being strategic means *taking the lead* in your career and your life. Being strategic means not waiting around for someone to notice you but instead determining what success looks like *for you* and then taking the necessary steps to get there."

When it comes to showing up strategic, there are two key areas most women should consider:

1. Enhancing their executive presence

2. Reframing their conversations

I know it might seem strange that these two factors are linked, but trust me—they are! Let's first look at how we can enhance our executive presence.

Showing Up Strategic with Executive Presence

Executive presence is an intangible trait that all successful leaders possess. At the senior ranks, everyone has technical competency, but not everyone has presence. Presence is the way you carry yourself—the persona that you convey in meetings and conversations. Is it really likely that people will judge you as being strategic just because you look and sound a certain way? While those things are a part of presence, they are not sufficient for appearing strategic. People make judgments at the unconscious level all the time. If you look and sound like you are strategic, people will give you the benefit of the doubt! On the other hand, *not* having executive presence can be a deal breaker and a key factor in determining whether you make it into the executive ranks.

The way you communicate is a huge part of executive presence. It's such a significant piece, in fact, that I will talk about it in depth in the next section. In the meantime, here are some additional ways to enhance your executive presence and appear more strategic:

- **Radiate confidence.** Confidence is one of the attributes most commonly considered a key component of executive presence. It is usually demonstrated by how much energy and passion you project to others, as well as how you present your ideas and opinions. Executives speak with a sense of authority and definitiveness by knowing their topic very well. They use voice inflections to stress key words such as using downward inflection (as opposed to a higher pitch) at the end of major phrases. And they speak slowly and mindfully and use the art of silence to bring their point home. Watch confident people in action and notice what they say and how they say it. Then find your own strategies and techniques for showing your confidence.
- **Listen before you advocate your position.** Listening is an art that truly successful executives value and master. Listening to what people are saying and recognizing what they are feeling about a situation before you try to convince them about something shows your respect and also helps you gain valuable information to build your case.
- **Be poised and centered at all times and especially in difficult situations.** Executives regularly face crises and stressful times—it's part of the job. In these situations, successful executives intentionally control their emotional reactions. They exhibit a sense of calmness and never overreact in the moment. They stay even-tempered, knowing that losing their

cool or appearing distraught can damage their reputation and effectiveness. They also do everything in their power to avoid taking criticism personally. Here are a few tips for staying poised in difficult situations:

○ **Count to 10 before you respond.** This may sound silly, but if you count to 10 before you respond, you will give yourself time to think and make a conscious choice in terms of what you say and do, rather than responding out of reaction.

○ **Listen for multiple "stories" with any situation.** When you are confronted with a difficult situation, try to gather a variety of perspectives on the subject. Don't assume that what you hear from one person will be the same as what you will hear from others. Try to get at the truth before you react to what might be a symptom of the problem rather than the core issue.

○ **Get curious rather than judgmental.** When we are judgmental—thinking something is right or wrong, good or bad, fair or unfair, etc.—we normally have an emotional reaction and we fail to gain the full information to make informed decisions.

○ **Consider "intention" separately from "impact."** When you are upset by something someone says or does, try to consider what that person meant the result to be and don't assume that it is the same as what the impact actually was. Sometimes we do and say something hoping for one result, but we get an entirely different one that is not what we ever intended. For example, suppose someone changes your slide deck hoping to improve it for you, and you are upset that some key information was left out. Before you voice your feelings about the situation, you might consider that the person was trying to help you, and thus you might use the situation as a coaching session rather than showing your frustration and criticizing the person. Again, when you do this, you give yourself a choice rather than just reacting in the moment.

- **Take credit where credit is due.** Julie Daum, coleader of the North American Board & CEO Practice at Spencer Stuart, shared with me that she thinks women often disempower themselves by not "owning" their accomplishments. She explained that "many women will do something significant and will give all the credit to their team without sharing [anything] about the role they had in the successful effort. And even if the woman does get credit for something, people seldom ever hear about what it took to get the job done. On the other hand, men will not hesitate to say, 'I wrote this' or 'I did this.' They always use the word 'I,' which they view as giving themselves the credit they deserve." To Julie's point, it's important to speak up and take credit for what you do so that people become aware of your effectiveness as a leader. It also helps to build the credibility and respect you deserve. In particular, when what you do impacts the business on a broader level, executives need to hear about it so that you get credit for working on a strategic level!

Showing Up Strategic in Conversations

To show up strategic, you have to "find your voice," which means being willing to speak up, to contribute, and to play an active role in leadership. You have to know and play to your strengths and be able to add value to the conversation. Here are some tips and techniques for finding your strategic voice:

- **Speak the language of business.** Caroline Leies, managing partner at MorganFranklin, shared, "It's important to talk about things in terms of tangible business and how your contribution links back to the numbers—the tangible impact around the business. By using the hard facts, no one can debate you." To Caroline's point, speaking like an executive means demonstrating your understanding of the entire enterprise and its intricate interconnectivity. You should have a solid understanding of what the other business functions do and how they do it. As well, you should have a working knowledge of finance—as it is often considered the official language of business. One of the best courses I took early on in my career was called Finance for Non-Financial Managers. Understanding business from that perspective is essential for any executive. Once you have this broader understanding of the business, you will intuitively speak more strategically because you will be thinking that way.

- **Connect to business strategy.** When you are sharing your point of view or introducing a new idea, be sure to link it to a specific business strategy. This will help you to create the impression that you are strategic, and it will also help you to garner support. Business strategies are focused on achieving business goals, and that's what executives are accountable for achieving.

    For example, I once coached a senior-level woman in human resources who was concerned about the recent results of an employee survey that indicated a decrease in employee satisfaction and morale, all leading to poor levels of engagement, which was directly impacting her organization's ability to keep and grow its talent. She had just presented her ideas on a potential solution to the board of directors, and she was not pleased with the board's reaction. She had opened her case by saying, "In order to attract, retain, and develop our talent, we need to create a corporate environment that is more inclusive and ensure that we have a learning culture for our employees." Imagine the reaction of the board members who were all "bottom-line" executives and who were primarily interested in how her ideas would impact the business!

We discussed what their reaction might have been if she had linked her opening statements to business goals and strategies. She could have said, "Given our company growth plan, our need for more talent, the labor shortage, and the trends related to gen X and gen Y—who are the future leaders of this business—we really have to think about human capital from a strategic standpoint now. Human capital is our greatest asset, and therefore it is our responsibility to create a culture of inclusion and a culture where continuous learning can support our innovative goals. This is what it is going to take to attract and retain a talented workforce that will continue to grow our business for years to come. What I'm going to talk about is how we can achieve this." Tying her ideas to something the members of her audience would recognize as a valuable business strategy would not only have gained their attention more effectively, but would also have created the impression that she was strategic.

- **Be clear and concise.** Being clear and concise when you speak is another way to demonstrate that you have executive presence and are in control of your messaging. Having clarity in what you say and how you say it means having a sense of purpose behind your words rather than filling the room with a stream of consciousness. Having clarity also means not wavering on your position just because it might not be popular. I think of Margaret Thatcher, who was the first female prime minister of England. Part of what got her to this high position was her clarity of purpose, speaking up when the odds were against her and never backing down. People respected her for it. She was also able to read her audience and tailor her message to what was important to her constituents in a way that made sense and gave them confidence in her as their leader. This is exactly what you want to be able to do.

For one-on-one daily conversations, being clear and concise primarily means getting to the point and not rambling. However, more thought and preparation is involved when you are addressing a group or an executive. Here are a few questions to ask yourself when you are preparing for an important conversation or meeting:

- *Why am I speaking and to whom?*
- *What do I hope to achieve? What do I already know about my audience? How can I gear what I say to my audience's level of understanding and interest?*
- *What do I want other people to think or do as a result of what I am going to say?*
- *How will I know if that happens? Why might they not want to think or do this?*
- *Why would they want to listen?*
- *What's in it for them? How can I link to something important or of value to them?*
- *How can I get others engaged in the conversation?*
- *What questions might I ask them to get their thoughts on the subject as well as to begin to gain their buy-in?*

- **Ask strategic questions.** Being strategic is not about replying immediately or jumping into the conversation in order to have your voice heard. More often, it's stepping back and asking a mindful question such as, "Can you share with me how this direction or initiative fits into our overall business strategy?" This shows that you are intelligent as well as strategic. To ask strategic questions, you must first do your homework. You have to learn all about your company as well as the market in which you are competing. And when you know enough, you will recognize the questions to ask that will demonstrate that you are able to think strategically.

Lota Zoth, a dear friend of mine who had been an executive in corporate America for many years and is now on several corporate boards, said that when you are an executive or are serving on a board, you get the most points for asking very thoughtful questions. She shared that once a CEO said to her, "Thanks for asking that question. I can't believe it, but no one has ever thought to ask me it before, and it's a great way to look at how integrative our strategy really is and where we might do better."

- **Become a good interpreter and storyteller.** The key to adding value when you brief an executive is to be an interpreter of the results or data you are presenting and make the connections to drive home the key messages or recommendations that matter most to him or her. Demystify and decomplexify the content and communicate using examples that listeners will remember.

Whether you are trying to explain something or get people to rally around your idea, the art of storytelling is one of the most effective ways to make a point. Lota Zoth said, "When developing a story for an audience, I try to find the commonality that puts us at the same level in terms of relationship. As an executive, it makes you human and helps others to connect with you." When you tell a story, be sure that it is relevant to the point you want to make and that it paints a picture that helps your audience better understand what you mean or validates what you are saying. Great leaders are often great storytellers, and this one particular skill can differentiate you from the pack. If you are effective at telling stories, you can actually be perceived as having a strategic mindset.

I often open up my talks on leadership with a personal story that is intended to not only capture the hearts of those in the audience, but also set the stage for my keynote message. One such story is about my first job out of college. I was the first woman to manage a production line at a particular General Motors plant. It was a blue-collar union environment, and I ran up against challenges and setbacks every day. I share how those early professional experiences shaped my belief systems and helped me develop a sense of self-awareness and confidence. I learned the importance of supportive relationships that ultimately were the key to my advancing in my career. This story resonates with audiences because other leaders can relate to getting out of their comfort zone, putting themselves in new experiences, and being willing to learn from those experiences.

This is just one example of storytelling. Everyone has a story. You have a story that people are curious about hearing. What story best defines you? Sharing a story with others is one way of connecting with others and building a sense of rapport and trust.

Be Innovative with Smart Power

At the personal level, being innovative means having the ability to continually learn new things and adapt to new situations in order to successfully navigate through complex change. It's hard to pick up a current business magazine without reading about how new demands, changes in organizational business models, and the emergence of a global economy all call for companies to acquire new knowledge that enables them to look at more innovative ways to grow, remain competitive, and prosper.

Essentially, in our current business environment, for women looking to advance in their career, this means having Smart Power, which is the capacity to create and sustain a broader learning environment within your team and your organization. So do you have Smart Power? Would you write Smart Power on your résumé as one of your key strengths? Probably not, as it is a relatively new term. But if I asked, "Are you a continuous learner?," how would you answer?

Being a continuous learner ensures that you will remain innovative, which is key to showing up strategic. Here are a few questions that might help you increase your Smart Power:

- **Are you aware of how others perceive you?** What did they think the last time you pitched an idea at a meeting? What did they think of your last presentation? How seriously do they take your ideas? How much influence do they think you have and with whom?
- **Are you aware of how others perceive your team?** What do people think of your team? Who on your team is being tapped to add additional value in other parts of the organization? What is your team getting credit for and with whom?
- **Do you look to other leaders as a source of new insights, fresh perspectives, and alternative strategies?** Do you have at least five or six mentors who can help you grow and develop? Are you constantly looking to see what you can learn from the folks that you are mentoring? Are you mentoring individuals on your team, and are you encouraging them to reach out for their own coaches and sponsors? Are they bringing new insights and experiences back to the team?
- **What are your aspirations for being an executive?** What are you doing to reach your goals? And who is helping you?

As you look at ways in which you can become a continuous learner and create a learning environment for your team, I want to remind you to use more of your innate abilities and connect them with your day-to-day roles as a leader.

Know Yourself and Leverage Your Natural Strengths

As a final thought about these keys to success, I encourage you not to dwell on how men succeed in business and, instead, focus your time and energy on what it will take for you to achieve your own personal career goals. Instead of competing with men on their terms, women must choose to take their own power and not apologize for showing up with their natural strengths that may indeed be different from those of their male colleagues. This can be challenging for women since leadership has historically been defined by men. This does not mean that some of the traits that are more masculine in nature are bad, an idea I dispelled earlier in the book; however, as we evolve into a new model of leadership thinking that integrates both the feminine and masculine (right and left) brain, I believe that women are naturally positioned to step in and help cultivate a better balance of leadership.

As you prepare for greater responsibility and visibility, be sure to show up with your intuition, collaborative style, empathy for others, integrated thinking, and focused purpose for what you are doing. While these are right-brain traits, it's important that you don't rule out or dismiss the left-brain traits that are also valuable. In my many years of experience coaching leaders and executives, I've found the most successful ones are those who can integrate their right- and left-brain thinking and surround themselves with people who complement both.

I had the pleasure of being the keynote speaker for VWR's National Women's Leadership Conference, and I was impressed to see several men in the room, since events like these are primarily attended by women. While most of the men were executive sponsors, I noticed that they were listening attentively while I was talking about the challenges women leaders face as well as the Sticky Floors that women sometimes experience. After my presentation, I followed up with Mark McLoughlin, senior vice president of Emerging Businesses at VWR, and we spoke about the importance of women showing up with their fully Integrated Leadership capacity.

Mark said, "I don't know of an organization that isn't heavily matrixed now, and that's where the collaborative skills, which many women do very well, become so critical. And you don't have to be a pushover to be collaborative." He continued, "I've been in this business for over 30 years, and I've had the opportunity to mentor and coach very talented women. What I found was that sometimes they were trying too hard to be tough, and it wasn't their predominant style, and so it didn't come off very well. I realize it's hard for women to decide sometimes how to show up and participate, particularly in a male-dominant environment, but as a guy, I thought it really took away from the skill sets that they had. I think the balance of being tough and collaborative is a really difficult line to walk, more so for a woman than a man. Maybe that's just my perspective, but the women I see advance to executive roles seem to have an authentic leadership style, and they are sincere about it. They're not overly brutal, which any gender can be, and they're not pushovers. They know how to balance it in a way that is comfortable for them, and they do it consistently."

What Mark is saying is very consistent with the premise of this book. We need more women in the executive ranks so that the natural perspectives and skills of both men and women, working together authentically, provide the best balance of leadership.

I still find women who feel uncomfortable showing up with their feminine traits as they look to advance to higher levels in the organization.

Here are some questions that might help you realize and tap into your Integrated Leadership capacity:

- What are your leadership principles when it comes to working with others? Do they align with the Integrated Leadership Model—using both your left- and right-brain traits?
- What are your personal strengths and talents—those areas that you are passionate about?
- What is the potential impact your strengths can create in the workplace? How can you leverage them?
- What holds you back from using your feminine leadership traits?
- What are the collective leadership traits (both right and left brain) that you can bring to your leadership team in order to have broader leverage and impact across your organization?
- What changes do you need to make to adjust your style and start using a broader suite of leadership styles?
- Are you using the full spectrum of leadership styles that will help you to advance to the next level of leadership?
- Where can you start using some of your other leadership styles that would be effective based on the situation?

We've talked about leveraging your power and showing up strategic in order to be considered a strong candidate for senior leadership positions. But it is difficult to do all this on your own. You really need mentors and sponsors to help you along the way, and so let's look at how to find and engage them!

Chapter Summary

- Women are strategic but often don't appear that way to others.
- When it comes to showing up strategic, most women should consider two key areas:

1. Enhancing their executive presence, including traits such as poise, confidence, and decision-making ability
2. Reframing their conversations—being willing to speak up, to contribute, and to play an active role in leadership

- Women leaders must have a solid understanding of all the major business functions as well as a working knowledge of finance, the official language of business.
- Women looking to advance their careers must have Smart Power—the capacity to create and sustain a broader learning environment within their team and organization.
- Instead of competing with men on their terms, women must know and leverage their unique gender strengths.

Chapter 15

Sponsorship Is Key for Advancement

A FORTUNE 500 CLIENT asked me recently to coach one of the firm's women leaders (I'll call her Susan), who was considered to be a rising star. Susan had interviewed for an executive position and hadn't been selected. Word was out that she might be considering another position with a competitor. She was very talented and would have been what we call a "regrettable loss" if she left the company. My client wanted to give her a coach, both to help her be better positioned for a promotion in the future and to keep her in his company.

When Susan and I spoke, she was very frustrated that she hadn't been selected because she felt she had the experience and skills that were required. She also had several mentors in the organization, who had given her advice about how to approach the interview, and she thought they would also put in a good word for her with the decision makers. While she thought the person selected was also qualified, she had no idea why that person was chosen instead of her.

We went down my checklist to see what she might have missed. She had documented her knowledge, skills, and abilities on her internal résumé as well as her key accomplishments and had discussed them in more detail during the interview. *Check.* She had described the unique value she would bring to the position and differentiated her-

171

self from other candidates. *Check*. She had mentioned the breadth and depth of her relationships—both inside and outside the organization. *Check*. And so on.

Finally, we got to my last question, "Who are your sponsors, and what exactly did they do to help you secure this promotion?" I got the same response to this question from Susan that I get from many very talented women who are stuck in middle management. She answered by describing her mentors to me and telling me how they had given her very helpful advice and taught her many valuable lessons. I asked again what they had said they would do specifically to help her win this new job, and she was at a loss. They had not volunteered to do anything, and she hadn't thought to ask for their help beyond their advice. She had never heard of the term *sponsor* . . . and that's where we began our work together!

According to SHAMBAUGH research, as well as other studies including "The Sponsor Effect: Breaking Through the Glass Ceiling," what propels women to the top of an organization is ultimately *sponsorship*. Sponsorship means that someone, at a high enough level to be influential, is committed to your becoming an executive. Without this, both men and women are likely to be overlooked for a promotion, regardless of their competence or performance—particularly at their midcareer point and beyond, where the competition for promotion increases.

When I interview women who have made it to the executive suite, I frequently hear about the people who helped them get to the top. These sponsors are executives who helped these women get recognized by senior staff, kept them in the loop about significant opportunities, and spoke on their behalf when promotions were available. Anne Altman, general manager of the Global Public Sector at IBM, shared with me, "The broader your responsibilities or the greater your accountability, the more important it becomes for others to know who you are, what you do, and why you are the best choice to advance to the next level." Anne also said that "sponsors are always thinking of ways they can 'up' the business, so they continuously are looking out for people that can bring unique skills and experiences to increase the value of the whole organization." As *you* move through the leadership pipeline, it's important to have a sponsor who has the positional power to help influence your advancement.

Sponsorship Versus Mentorship

When I speak at a women's leadership conference, I always ask the members of the audience how many of them have mentors, and usually more than half the members raise their hands. But when I ask how many have sponsors, I'm surprised if I see more than four or five hands in the air. You see, women are excellent at relationship building, and they are finally getting the courage to ask for mentoring. But when it comes to asking executives to go to bat for them and serve as a dedicated advocate to help advance them into the senior ranks, they aren't doing it for two main reasons. First, they don't know that they need advocacy, and second, they don't know how to ask for it. And that's exactly what this chapter is all about!

Do you know the difference between a mentor and a sponsor? A mentor is someone who acts as a role model and close advisor. Mentors provide a helpful perspective on how to invigorate your career, how to achieve internal recognition, how to navigate the political waters, and so on. They are a tremendous resource for your overall development, and everyone should have a few. However, rarely do they engage in conversations where they are advocating for you.

Sponsors, on the other hand, do a lot of what mentors do, but they take it to the next level and are willing to speak positively on your behalf. They will promote your visibility and strongly recommend you for strategic opportunities, even by "calling in their chips" on your behalf. Finally, they will directly connect you with others who can help to further your career and grease the skids for your advancement. They essentially feel that they succeed if you advance.

Many surveys indicate that high-potential women are *overmentored* and *undersponsored* relative to their male peers, and this is a key reason why they are not advancing in their organizations. In the 2008 Catalyst survey, 83 percent of women and 76 percent of men said they had at least one mentor at some point in their career, and 21 percent of women said they had four or more mentors, compared with 15 percent of men. Although more women than men had mentors, the women's mentors had less organizational clout. In fact, 78 percent of the men, as indicated in this particular Catalyst study, were actively mentored by a CEO or another senior executive, whereas women had junior-level mentors. Also, 7 percent of women were mentored by a nonmanager or a first-level manager, compared with only 4 percent of men.

So what's wrong with this picture? I think there are basically three issues that we need to address.

First, it's human nature to seek advice from people who are like us, and consequently men seek out men and women seek out women in most mentoring relationships. This is a problem for women, based on the limited number of women at the top, which reduces the number of executive women available to be sponsors. So, by default, women tend to have male mentors rather than female mentors.

The second issue for women is how they leverage their mentors. When I ask men and women how their mentors have been valuable to them, men will commonly reply that they asked their mentors to use their political clout and endorse the men publicly for specific opportunities. Women say that they valued their mentor's advice on leadership approaches to a situation, work-life challenges, or ways they could further develop professionally. They often cite homework assignments and "lessons learned" as the value-added component of their mentoring experience. Even when women have been matched up with senior-level male mentors, usually as part of a corporate mentoring program, few have ever asked their mentor to advocate for them.

The third issue is that women, even when given the chance, typically don't ask for help in advancing their career due to their beliefs and assumptions. When I question women about why they don't specifically ask for sponsorship, I often hear that it seems manipulative to them. They think they should be able to be successful on their own rather than because they asked someone to advocate for them. It's as if they don't realize that men do this for each other all the time! I also hear from women that it's too risky. Women fear that their mentors will think they are not confident enough or that their mentors will say no—which translates to the fear of rejection.

The broader issue here is that while women are comfortable asking for help for their colleagues and team members, it seems to be more difficult for them to ask for what they want or need for themselves. This shows up in a variety of situations. I recently met with a female executive who was hiring several new team members at a very senior level. What stood out for her after the interview process was that every man she made an offer to would ask for a signing bonus or particular job title with some kind of higher salary package. However, when she made offers to women, their response was how grateful they were to work with her, and they completely passed up asking for additional perks or monies. Women will have to push through this Sticky Floor of not asking for what they want or need in order to turn their mentors into sponsors.

Invest in Relational Capital

In the "Sponsor Effect" study, the authors use the term *relational capital* as a core reason why men have more sponsors than women. Having relational capital means having a broad network of people around you to gain support and cooperation for the important goals and objectives you are trying to accomplish. When you get higher up in the organization, you only have the top 10 percent of performers in the talent pool. When CEOs or other very senior executives need to promote someone, they generally turn back to their inner circle and ask their peers for recommendations—which candidates would they feel comfortable promoting?

Unfortunately, many women resist the idea that it's the people you know that really count, clinging instead to the belief that promotions are a result of accomplishments and hard work. In research conducted by Catalyst, 77 percent of women employees indicated that they believe what drives promotions in their firm is a combination of hard work, long hours, and educational credentials. On the other hand, 83 percent of men indicated that in terms of advancement, the people you know count at least as much as your skill and competence in doing your job. Very different perspectives!

While women are known for their ability to build and nurture relationships, they fail to cultivate and invest in relational capital. (Men, on the other hand, seem to have mastered this brilliantly!) Women build relationships with people who can help them do their current job well, rather than developing relationships with key decision makers who will ultimately help them get promoted. As indicated in *Harvard Business Review*'s "*Harvard Business Review* Research Report," a mere 14 percent of full-time female employees in large companies have sponsors, compared with 46 percent of men who are likely to have a sponsor. Part of this is due to women not investing in relational capital. If this is true of you, it's time to start identifying and cultivating a potential sponsor. You need to start thinking broader and bigger. Sometimes it calls for getting out of your comfort zone and building relationships with people specifically for this purpose.

Build and Leverage a Meaningful Network

In *It's Not a Glass Ceiling, It's a Sticky Floor*, I explore several areas where women hold themselves back from advancing in their career, but one of the biggest Sticky Floors in terms of reaching the executive suite is not building a strategic network and using it with intention. The key to finding a sponsor is first cultivating a rich and diverse network of executives (both men and women). The data show that leaders who consistently rank in the top 20 percent of their companies, in both *performance* and *well-being*, have a diverse but select network of relationships. People in their network come from several different spheres both inside and outside their organizations.

Building a network isn't an overnight process. You can't just walk up to people and ask them to be your sponsor. Normally, the folks you want to sponsor you are senior-level staff, who have credibility and influence. Clients can be strong sponsors if they have a relationship with a key executive in your company. You just have to be politically correct in how you go about cultivating their advocacy.

In order for potential sponsors to buy into you and want to support your advancement, they have to get to know you as a person and then learn more about your career goals as well as your unique value proposition. One way to start building this relationship is by finding a way to get in front of them, such as working on a task force or engaging in a social event that a particular individual sponsors.

Let me share a personal example of how this worked for me. Several years ago, I met someone (who turned out to be my sponsor) by playing in a charity golf event. By no means was I a great golfer, but I took a few lessons so I could at least play a respectable game. I was put in a foursome that included Jack, a client I admired and had always wanted as an internal advocate for me with this particular client.

After the game, I headed to the reception, where Jack came up to me and said that I played a great game (I think he was impressed with my drive off the tee!). That broke the ice, and we began to talk more about what I did for his company, including the fact that I was a coach for some of the executives. Jack was very curious about the coaching that I was doing and said that he had one person on his team that he needed to follow up with regarding his performance review. It was not going to be an easy conversation, and he asked for ideas on how to get prepared and approach the conversation. I shared with him a coaching framework that is particularly helpful in giving and receiving feedback, especially in difficult conversations.

To make a long story short, he and I got to know each other, and he became my biggest fan in his organization; and as a result of his sponsorship, SHAMBAUGH has had a lasting relationship with his company. The fact that Jack wanted to champion me and my company had less to do with my golf game and more to do with the fact that I put myself out there where the big boys played, and as a result, I had the opportunity to build a strategic relationship that was a win-win for both of us. Sometimes you have to earn the right to get to know someone by putting yourself in a situation where you meet influential people and creating the opportunity for yourself. Not every attempt will find you that special sponsor, but if you don't make the effort, sponsors are not going to come looking for you!

In SHAMBAUGH's Women in Leadership and Learning Program, we spend time exploring the benefits of having a strategic network and the importance of having connections with senior-level men. When helping women expand their network, we ask them to think about it as a web of connections that leads to a broader and richer set of relationships. The relationships we are talking about are multidimensional. Every person in your network has his or her own network that you can tap into. When the women begin to map out their existing web, many of their relationships are narrow in nature, meaning they are within their functional area or team. Their connections are usually people they know very well and have had long-term and trusted relationships with. Few are with men and even fewer with executive men and women.

In order to strategically expand and leverage your network, you must first analyze your current network. The following chart is a tool we use that helps people to view their network less as a one-to-one network and more as a multidimensional one. We refer to this tool in

SHAMBAUGH's Women's Leadership Program as Your Web of Connections, which you can tap for gaining support with key goals and objectives and particularly for helping you to advance in your career.

Here are a few questions to get you started:

- Are most of your relationships within your team or functional area, or are they spread out across the company?
- How many (if any) executives do you have in your network?
- How many men at the senior level are you connected with?
- Who in your network might know people who could be your sponsor?
- What percentage of the relationships are on the inside versus outside of your company? (You want sponsors in both areas.)
- Who do you know that might introduce you to a potential sponsor in a client organization?

Identify and Capitalize on Sponsors

Based on the questions you just answered, I hope you have started thinking about ways to expand your network. When planning your new web of relationships, the one that will lead you to sponsorship, the first step is to ask yourself what your career goals are, what needs to happen to achieve them, and who can help you. Next, think about who else needs to be in your network now, as well as who it is that you currently know and might tap as a sponsor. When you have these people identified, the next step is to put a strategy together to cultivate a sponsor relationship. Here are a few tips for doing this.

Know What You Want in Terms of Your Career

Having a sponsor is necessary only if you have specific career goals and are determined to achieve them. You need to know what you want in order to determine whom you need to help you get it. Begin by writing down a career goal you want to achieve in the next year. This will help you to be intentional about seeking out the right people to have in your network. And remember, your career goal may change as time goes by, but having a goal is essential for putting a plan together to find and leverage sponsors.

Consider Potential Sponsors

Once you have your goal in mind, consider people who are already in your network that you might convert to sponsors. They should have credibility and influence and be connected to the senior staff in some way—either they are executives themselves, or they "have the ear" of senior staff. Look around. Whom haven't you thought about? Think beyond your own web of connections and share your career goals with others who can suggest sponsors to you.

And don't forget that your current mentors can become sponsors. Keep in mind that while mentors are giving you advice, you should also be telling them about your successes and your aspirations. Karen Dahut, senior vice president of Booz Allen Hamilton, said:

> Many women say they struggle with how to change the game in mentoring relationships. Women naturally fall into a mentee role, asking "How am I doing? What can I do to improve? How did I perform in that last meeting?"
>
> That's all fine, but they also need to be saying, "Look at what I'm doing . . . Look at the things that I have on my plate . . . I've got this strategy for . . . I'm executing this plan in order to . . . I'm developing these people . . ." But we so rarely talk to mentors that way. We are more comfortable seeking advice and counsel. My advice to women is always to make your mentor your champion.

So be sure you are having the right kind of conversations with your mentors as you explore the possibility of turning them into your sponsors! Also it's essential to have a proven track record with these folks, meaning that you have delivered great results for them in the past and they are happy with what you have done. People need to believe in you if they are going to sponsor you.

Put Yourself Out There to Engage Them

Once you've identified several people who might be potential sponsors, you need to figure out how to get on their radar and build a relationship with them. Ask yourself what you are willing to do to get in front of that person. Whom might you know to ask for an introduction? What events does the person speak at, or what committees does he or she sit on? The bottom line is that you need to figure out where and how you can get access to this person. At the end of the day, this often involves doing things that don't come naturally for many women. But if you really want to become an executive, you need to be able to do this, and I suggest that you live with the discomfort and do it anyway! Know that each time you reach out to someone, it will become easier the next time. You will learn what works best for you, and eventually you will begin to do it intuitively.

I mentioned that clients can be effective sponsors. Getting involved at the senior levels with folks outside your organization can help you to gain credibility as an industry expert, which helps to differentiate you and build trust with your executives. It also helps you expand your contacts within the industry and tap into a broader base of business relationships. Attending industry events, making presentations, or publishing within your industry is a great way to be recognized as a thought leader, which you can then bring inside the company to gain greater credibility with the CEO and his or her team. People outside your organization who think highly of you provide what we call indirect sponsorship. You just have to be sure they share their opinion of you with the right people inside your company!

Ask for What You Want!

When I spoke with Tory Johnson, CEO of Women for Hire, I asked her what she felt were the most self-limiting factors for women when it comes to advancing in their career. She said, "I think it's being clear about what you want and recognizing that you've got to be self-directed to get it. We still have this idea that if we just do a good job, someone's going to tap us on the shoulder and reward us with a promotion, and that so rarely happens. You can't wait. Nobody's coming to save you. It's up to you and you alone to put together a plan and then rally the right people to mentor and sponsor you. But most important, you have to know what you want and what specifically you want each person to do for you. You can't expect them to be able to read your mind. Then you have to have the courage to actually ask them to do it."

Dana Moruzzi, vice president of Portfolio Lead, Biotech, at VWR, said, "I think women sometimes view asking for help as a sign of weakness, and it's not that at all. If anything, I think it actually works to our advantage. Reaching out to a man and asking for help can be a good thing. The men I ask to help me are usually flattered. They are very willing to coach or mentor me, and many have willingly sponsored me when I put it out there. I think most people feel good if someone reaches out to them like this."

When you are asking for help or sponsorship, clarity is important. If you have reached out to individuals and they have said no to your request or indicated that they would help but then didn't, it's probably because you were not clear up front about what you were looking for and how they could help you. So the clearer and more direct you are with your ideas, the easier you make it for the other person. Here are a few tips to consider when preparing for the "ask" with your potential sponsor:

- Be clear about what you are looking for in the sponsor relationship. Engage in fundamental conversations about your career aspirations and be specific about where you need help.
- When stating your request, connect it to how it would be good for the business.
- Communicate why you think this individual is the right person to help you.
- Be sure you gain agreement regarding exactly what this person will do for you and don't assume anything.
- If the person doesn't feel he or she is able (or willing) to help you, be OK with it. There are lots of potential sponsors out there!

Finally, when you are talking to a potential sponsor, have strength and conviction about your value equation as well as your career goals. Here are a few points to consider that can help you develop your message:

- What is your unique value?
- What successes have you had in the last three to six months?
- What makes you great at what you do?
- What do you love about your work?
- Who is your "best self" that you want others to know about?
- What messages are most likely to help you achieve advocacy from this person?
- What are the limits of your comfort zone, and how far out of it can you stretch in order to gain this person's sponsorship?

For those of you who are working long hours and driving home late every night, think about the individuals who are getting the promotions. While they may also be putting in long hours, there is a very good chance that their promotions have a lot to do with the quality of their network, being intentional in requesting advocacy and using their connections to advance their career.

Build Relationship Intimacy

We've talked about building and leveraging your strategic network in order to develop sponsorship for yourself, and now I'd like to focus on an aspect of relationship building that is key to achieving this unique kind of support. People generally won't advocate for you unless they feel that you both know each other very well. While you want them to know about your strengths and particular value equation, as well as the ways your advancement will benefit them and the organization, it's also important for you to understand their business, what success looks like to them and what their constraints are. We call this mutual understanding and genuine concern for each other *relationship intimacy*.

Karen Dahut, the executive at Booz Allen Hamilton whom I mentioned earlier, said, "When cultivating a sponsor relationship, I don't shy away from asking them for their advice and mentorship. But I also work hard to be of value on their behalf." One example Karen gave was when she was looking to evolve a male executive mentor into a sponsor and she began to think of ways that she could support him. Karen has a strong background in finance, which was an area this particular executive didn't know much about. She reached out to him and suggested that she serve as his unofficial CFO for one of his key projects. Karen said, "That was both an opportunity for him to mentor me and for him to see me in action."

Karen is suggesting that one of the best ways to convert mentors to sponsors is for them to see you in action so that they can tell others about you based on firsthand experience. As Karen said, "How can someone really advocate for you if they've never seen you in action?" Whether it's through meetings with that person or through initiatives they're driving, working on their behalf is a key strategy for building trust and fostering an advocate.

Here are a few tips for how to cultivate a sponsor relationship so that it's a win-win:

- Building a level of intimacy calls for making sure potential sponsors know about you, but it's just as important that you know what's important to them. Take time to understand their goals and constraints.
- Find out what success looks like to them, whether it's a promotion, recognition, client reputation, visibility, thought leadership, etc.

- Be proactive and look for ways you can be of value to them.
- Find ways for them to see you in action so that you will earn their respect and trust as well as give them stories to tell about you.

Give Men a Chance!

If you have a majority of women in your network and as your mentors, it's not necessarily a bad thing, because women naturally know how to connect with each other, and they can often empathize with your world better than men can. However, don't forget that it's important to balance your network with men. They still hold the majority of executive positions and have the clout to make things happen (or not happen) in regard to your career.

As I mentioned, I've found men very willing to help when I've been clear about what I want them to do. They don't seem to respond as well to indirect requests or vague messages, and so being clear and concise with them is essential. One approach I've used successfully is to "consult" with them. This is where you explain a situation or problem and ask for their advice. Then you conclude with a specific request—asking them to do something for you that involves advocacy. And while this request for sponsorship only pertains to a particular situation, you will actually begin to build a bridge for future requests. This is why it's important for you to be thinking about how you can bring value in return—so you can reciprocate. This is what builds *relationship intimacy* in the long term.

Help Other Women Along the Way

Invariably when I'm speaking at a women's leadership conference, I get asked, "Are women harder on other women?" Over the course of my career, I have had the good fortune to have had supportive women colleagues and bosses. However, I also often hear about how women struggle with their female bosses or how other women sabotage them or talk poorly about them in conversations with their colleagues. In fact, there have been several studies that indicate that more than 50 percent of men and women agreed that women are harder on other women in the workplace than they are on men.

Gail Evans, former CNN executive, diversity expert, and author and speaker on women's issues, shared with me, "The big message for women is that we all have to play this game together. Women are not as good as men in supporting each other. As a result, we sabotage each other, and ultimately that's not going to get us where we want to be." And I agree. We say we want more women in executive positions, more female executives to mentor and sponsor other women, and then, when we have the chance, we do nothing to make it happen—or worse yet, do something to make sure it doesn't happen. Instead of buying into the cultural and gender biases that are still alive and well in some organizations, we need to be agents for change.

One of the first things we can do is watch how we talk about other women. Be sure you speak to their strengths and give them the credit and opportunities they deserve. It's also important for us to look at ways to mentor or sponsor other women. I invite you to be an inspiration for other women. Every day you have an impact on women who are aspiring leaders. The saying "It takes a village" is so true, and women need to be truly supportive of one another. Be open and reach out to women when you can lend some advice, advocate, or sponsor them for a promotion or board seat. If you are in an influential role and you don't see women moving through the leadership pipeline, be the one in a room who pushes back and says there's something wrong. And if you are the only female executive in the company, go to your human resource or talent management team and ask the people there to find more women to assume senior leadership roles in your organization.

Be assured that the younger generations are watching those of us currently in executive roles. The signals we send about how we support other women and how we lead with our authentic self not only are important to each of us but will also be critical to the women who choose to join our organizations in the future . . . some of whom may be our daughters or nieces!

Chapter Summary

- Surveys indicate that high-potential women are *overmentored* and *undersponsored* relative to their male peers, and this is a key reason why they are not advancing.
- Many women resist the idea that "who you know" makes a difference.
- It's crucial that women have a sponsor who has the positional power to help influence a promotion and that they know how to leverage that sponsor appropriately. Tips for gaining sponsorship include:
  - Cultivate and invest in relational capital by building relationships with key decision makers who can help you advance
  - Build and leverage a meaningful network
  - Identify and capitalize on potential sponsors
  - Take time to build relationship intimacy
  - Balance your network with both male and female mentors and sponsors
  - Support, mentor, and sponsor other women

Part III Summary

Women's natural strengths and style are needed to find the right harmonious balance for leadership today and in the future. Men can't do it alone. Women are a crucial part of the leadership equation, which means they need to not only realize their important role, but also get off their Sticky Floors and tap into all their leadership capacity. In order to see more women in executive roles, women have to first see themselves in the executive suite and then believe that they can be promoted to those positions whether their leadership is in an organization, in public service, or in their communities. It's all about being the change you want to see and not waiting for someone to make it happen for you.

When I speak to women around the country, I feel a sense of energy and optimism. Women are realizing that they have the power and talent to be an important part of the leadership equation. There is a growing expression of "sisterhood," and women are reaching out to other women and supporting one another more than ever before. This in no way means that men are out of the picture or that women believe they can do this on their own. Rather, women are seeing their own gifts and gaining the confidence and competence to step into their power and be good integrators with men.

In closing this section, I invite you to answer these questions in order to trigger your intentionality:

- Do you have any false assumptions or myths about being an executive?
- Do you know what you want in terms of your career, and do you have a plan to get there?

- Are you on the right escalator to take you where you want to go in your career?
- Are you aware of your Sticky Floors, and are you systematically addressing them?
- How can you more fully leverage your Personal Power base through knowledge, leadership persona, resilience, and communication?
- How can you more fully leverage your Organizational Power through your role, resources, network, and reputation?
- Do you use your power to do the right thing or make a difference for those around you?
- Are you showing up to others as strategic or tactical?
- What can you do to enhance your executive presence and communication effectiveness?
- Do you recognize your strengths, and are you socializing your value equation with the right people?
- Are you clear on what "success" looks like for you, and do you have the right people in your network to help you get there?
- Do you have the courage to get out of your comfort zone to grow, learn, reach your fullest potential, and gain sponsorship?
- Do you have at least two or three strong sponsors? Are you leveraging your mentors so that they will sponsor you?
- Are you tapping the right people—men throughout your organization and both male and female executives?
- Are you open to men being your sponsor, and do you embrace the qualities and support they can provide?
- Do you reach out and support other women, intentionally looking at ways to help advance women around you?

Part IV

Integrated Leadership: The Organization's Role

Chapter 16

Organizations Can Make It Happen

WHILE INDIVIDUAL men and women leaders are on the front lines when it comes to creating an Integrated Leadership team, the importance of the organization and its top leadership can't be underestimated. To leverage the full potential of the Integrated Leadership Model, organizations must be committed to advancing women through the leadership pipeline—all the way to the top! In order for this to happen, organizations and their leaders must build a strong business case, create an inclusive culture, and continue to encourage and develop all their potential leaders.

For organizations that want to develop an Integrated Leadership Model, I recommend a systematic approach that uses the company's HR strategies (succession planning, talent management programs, measurement and recognition programs, leadership development process, etc.) as a foundation and focuses on individual leaders, teams, and the organization as a whole.

Steps in the Systematic Approach for Organizations

1. Build and Communicate Your Business Case

Failure to have a business case for Integrated Leadership is the biggest reason why companies are maintaining the status quo in terms of filling senior leadership positions. And having a solid business case doesn't mean just knowing the business case either. Executives need to talk about the business case frequently and everywhere they go so that it's wired into everyone's thinking. I advise companies to link their business case for Integrated Leadership to their leaders' goals and to the success of the business so that the process moves beyond conversation and to intentional action.

I have already presented a number of facts and research on the "why" for Integrated Leadership at the beginning of this book, and I encourage you to look back at the compelling statistics. However, it is crucial that you identify the business case that is most relevant and compelling for your organization and your unique situation.

For example, if you are a senior leader in an organization, you should know how the marketplace shifts and how your company needs to tap into the perspectives and views of women. I was amazed when I recently read that 91 percent of women say they felt misunderstood based on how products and services were being marketed to them through advertising. That can translate into a huge business loss since women are 85 percent of our consumer base right now. Can you see the great business case for having more women in these industries making key decisions about their products with that in mind!

One of the best business cases I've seen recently is tied to the need for innovation in almost every industry. It seems to be a critical factor for competitive advantage now and in the future. And what drives innovation? It's driven by diversity of thought and perspective at all levels across all disciplines in the organization.

Dr. Katherine Frase, vice president of Industries Research at IBM, said, "To be an innovative and successful organization in today's economy, you need to have a culture that doesn't focus just on the end result, but also on the process of how you got there—which speaks to the importance of multiple ways of thinking about and approaching problems and opportunities." This is a situation where having more women in senior leadership—and therefore a more balanced leadership team—can definitely help.

Ana Duarte-McCarthy, chief diversity officer at Citi Group, offered another good example of a strong business case for establishing Integrated Leadership and investing in women at Citi. She said, "An important aspect of looking at helping women to advance in the organization connects to Citi's retention model, which is really important to our business. When a highly regarded woman leaves the firm, it reverberates in an organization because all the women we view as high potentials are in very significant roles. When people leave Citi, they take important client relationships with them. They are also revenue producers and have equity in terms of our brand, which they also take with them." Ana also said that when someone who's covering a major financial institution leaves Citi, that creates a gap of institutional knowledge, which understandably has a negative impact.

Ana shared, "We look at our development programs for women as something that's going to move the business strategy forward. So it's not a 'nice to do.' And I think it's similar to what you'd find at many firms—it's moved from being a compliance activity to a business imperative. Therefore we are always asking ourselves: Are we supporting talent? Are we moving talent forward? Are we looking at how we fill opportunities? And are we looking at progress that's made against those actions, so that people understand that it is something that is part of our broader vision of getting the best and brightest?" Bottom line and to Ana's point, the loss of a knowledgeable and experienced leader, man or woman, can translate into what I refer to as a "regrettable loss" and can have significant impact from a financial and competitive-advantage perspective, which has merit for linking back to an organization's business case.

These are just a few examples of how to think about a business case. I'm sure you can think of others related to your core business.

2. Create an Inclusive Corporate Culture

The good news is that companies are starting to catch on and CEOs are realizing that to continue to grow in their marketplace, attract and keep good talent, and maintain their competitive edge, they need a rich pool of diverse perspectives and ideas. And they realize that the culture of their business is an important factor in this equation.

I interviewed a dear colleague of mine, Anne Reed, chairman of the board for ASI Government (formerly Acquisition Solutions). Anne felt strongly that a big factor for ASI Government ensuring success was based on the culture it created from its early conception of the company. Anne commented:

> I have always felt like the businesses that are most successful have the most balance, and that they're gender balanced and diverse across multiple perspectives, which brings a unique diversity of thinking. Today, there's so much competition, that successful businesses have to differentiate themselves. I think the way to do that is to successfully harness the creative powers and the more directive/analytic skills that people have and find that new balance.
>
> What fosters this unique and very powerful synergy of diverse intelligence was the culture that we created early on. It is a culture that respects different opinions and the professionalism that everybody brings to the table. There's no single individual that has created a domineering perspective—we've tried to avoid the culture of "yes." Everybody comes together and everybody shares. Decisions do get made, not everything is decided by committee, but we have created a freedom for people to bring forward their best thinking

and to initiate a dynamic of conversation—whether it's about business strategy or what our policies ought to be with respect to our employees, or how we're going to approach a particular bid on new business opportunities. There's a willingness to participate. People enjoy the free exchange of ideas.

To Anne's point, one of the first and most important things a company can do for creating and leveraging the Integrated Leadership Model is create a culture that gives permission and embraces unique and different views and perspectives. Anne said, "There is a cultural norm when hiring into the company, and that is whatever your gender, race, age, or perspective you bring to the table, it's valued and people are encouraged to show up with their 'true' self and thinking."

SHAMBAUGH has worked with a number of organizations in helping them to develop and implement a framework that not only has positive and lasting results in advancing women and minorities, but also fosters a culture of accountability that links to the company's business outcomes.

In an interview on Bloomberg News, Jim Turley, CEO of Ernst & Young, indicated that having greater diversity is key to the company's business. Jim said, "Very soon, 75 percent of our customers as well as our workers will not be white males." Jim also said, "Today's companies will risk falling behind if they don't start engaging more women and a more diverse team of men. And it needs to start at the top. This calls for holding our practice leaders accountable and also building a corporate culture that empowers and enables this particular mix of individuals to work effectively together."

To elaborate on what Jim said, without men and women working toward the goal of leadership that embraces the best knowledge skills, abilities, and traits of *all leaders*, and without organizations establishing a culture that encourages and sustains this, companies will continue trying one quick fix after another and will find themselves trailing the more innovative companies of the world.

Sodexo is a good example of how to create an inclusive corporate culture. With a strategic focus on how diversity can drive employee engagement and impact business development, the company created an initiative called Making Every Day Count.

This initiative was designed to provide the tools, resources, and support necessary to ensure the success of all employees, including women. With a strategic focus on the business case and how diversity can drive employee engagement and business development, Sodexo's diversity efforts have developed from a compliance framework to a strategic business imperative embedded in the fabric of the culture.

The initiative leverages a host of professional development programs that present opportunities to share diversity lessons with staff and clients, provide training to different employee populations, and develop connections through strategic networking and robust mentoring. The initiative focused on Sodexo's 15,000-plus salaried employees working at 6,000 client sites and offices throughout the United States. It leveraged a top-down, bottom-up, middle-out strategy to drive diversity and inclusion in every Sodexo office.

The strategic nature of this initiative has produced strong results. Overall, from 2003 to 2010, the number of women in leadership positions at Sodexo has increased by 74 percent. During this same time period, the number of women on the executive committee increased from three to five. Women's share of positions in the executive pipeline increased from 23 to 33 percent, with the "racially-ethnically diverse" women's share increasing from 6 to 9 percent. In addition, in 2010, engagement scores for women were at 71 percent, up 10 percent from 2006—which is considered above the AON Hewitt threshold for "best in class."

3. Build and Leverage Gender Intelligence

The first step to ensure you have a broad spectrum of gender intelligence is to raise awareness about the different ways that men and women think, make decisions, negotiate, communicate, and resolve conflicts.

Without this broad understanding and appreciation for these differences, men and women will continue to hit an impasse in terms of valuing and capitalizing on their differences. Women will not be seen as having executive potential if men continue to look for executives who think and act like them. And men will not be able to promote women if the women in these companies do not make their goals clear. The broader spectrum of thinking will be blocked, and this will stall innovation. The good news is that once men and women understand their differences, begin to value them, and learn how to adapt to them, they begin to realize the benefits of gender balance.

Here's an example of how a company fostered awareness of gender intelligence. Several years ago, Deloitte & Touche realized that just hiring more women would not address the retention issue it had with its women leaders. Deloitte & Touche realized that it needed to deal with the fundamental differences in how men and women think and approach issues. Women were leaving the company primarily because they were not being promoted to more senior roles. Part of the problem was when male executives got ready to advance someone into a senior role, they were not aware of the unique strengths women brought to the position. Also, even though the women were getting great business results, the senior men didn't feel comfortable with the style of women in a predominantly male environment.

Studies have found that many women who have been promoted to executive roles felt as though they needed to show up using masculine traits and styles, leaving their natural strengths at the front door. Many felt that they weren't heard, and for that reason, they chose to leave the company.

In Deloitte & Touche's case, the company realized that the lack of gender awareness was directly impacting its ability to attract, advance, and retain talented women. It rolled out a professional development program that specifically addressed the gender intelligence gap. These sessions helped men and women to understand the gender-related thinking and communication styles and to value their unique differences. For men, in particular, the sessions helped them realize their blind spot when it came to seeing women's strengths and the unique value they brought to the business. For women, this training gave them permission to be their authentic selves in the workplace!

Building and leveraging gender awareness also calls for organizations to help managers and leaders with their hardwired biases and stereotyping. It's important to have programs that get to the core of stereotyping and help people explore their unconscious biases. These programs need to provide the tools and techniques to help them reframe their beliefs and assumptions about people who are different from them. Here are some of the topics that should be included in these types of programs:

- **Gender differences.** Addressing differences in thinking, communicating, making decisions, solving problems, negotiating, and resolving conflicts
- **The value of difference.** Learning how to embrace and integrate differences in daily work activities and with clients
- **Overcoming gender biases.** Gaining an understanding of one's biases and testing them against a new reality
- **Gender intelligence and clients.** Building stronger customer relationships and increasing loyalty by leveraging gender strengths
- **Promoting innovation.** Fostering diversity of thought to spark creativity

4. Advance Your Talent Through Sponsorship

One of the most effective ways to advance your top talented women leaders and minorities is through sponsorship. Ana Duarte-McCarthy at Citi shared with me that Citi has put in place an initiative that aligns the company's top talented women with senior executives who become their advocates. This sponsorship program was created specifically with the objective of identifying high-potential women already in fairly senior roles who are deemed as ready to move to a next job and who are interested in mobility. Each of the women is paired with an executive sponsor (male or female) who is viewed as influential at Citi. Citi also provides each of the women with a coach, along with assessments to help better define areas each woman wants to work on.

I asked Ana about the overall progress Citi is making with its sponsorship program, and she replied, "It's making a difference for these women already, as people are talking about them; they'll be specifically part of the conversation at our annual talent review. I think it's also a great way for the companies to say to the employees, 'We want to invest in you, and we are investing in your talent, your capacity, and your future.' I think this is a great way for Citi to say, 'We're betting on your potential.' What a great message that is to get, by the way, right?"

Ana also said that accountability is important, and so is having the C-suite engaged. For example, Ana said, "Citi launched Citi Women, our global women's initiative to support the advancement of women in 2006. CEO Vikram Pandit is committed to Citi Women. His endorsement is very important; otherwise it would feel like another program of the month."

Finally, Ana said that another benefit of this initiative is that executives are motivated to help these individuals, as they get a lot out of being advocates. Ana noted, "They get great insight into the business, because now they're meeting with people probably a little deeper in the organization, so they're getting good business insight about the organization. They have an opportunity to develop their own coaching skills, and I think there is a sense of doing something good that's contributing to the development of talent, and they're playing a pivotal role in that. It's terrific."

Ernst & Young has also had success advancing women to the senior levels through a targeted program that created greater access and mentoring opportunities with their senior executives, which the company calls the Inclusive Leadership Program. This program creates formal mentoring relationships by pairing women with Ernst & Young's Americas Executive Board members and an external coach to ensure that Ernst & Young is fully capitalizing on the talent available in its leadership ranks. After creating a customized development plan based upon results of 360-degree feedback, women work with their mentor and executive coach to execute that plan. It is not your typical mentoring program, because Americas Executive Board members are the highest-ranking leaders in the Americas of Ernst & Young.

Karyn Twaronite, partner and Americas inclusiveness officer at Ernst & Young, explained to me, "We realized that we didn't have enough women attaining account and titled leadership roles, such as those running big divisions with P&Ls. In response, we launched the 'Inclusiveness Leadership Program' in 1999 to engage a group of women partners in a three-year program. This particular program has helped to better position these women when it comes time for our board to make key promotion and assignment decisions. It basically levels the playing field because men typically have had access to other male partners and to this particular board, whereas the women partners did not necessarily have this access. Consequently, these board mentors knew the women just as well as they knew the men, which greatly helped the women's advancement. When we started this program, only 6 percent of women held titled leadership roles, and then in 2004 it went up to 15 percent. Last year women attained 18 percent of Ernst & Young's partner/principal population and 21 percent of titled leadership roles in the Americas. And now 27 percent of Americas subarea managing partners—who manage the 11 biggest P&Ls—are women."

Based on SHAMBAUGH's work in this area, I believe we will see more of these types of sponsorship and mentorship programs within organizations. What's key is that they provide greater visibility, exposure, and opportunities for their top talented women, and there is a commitment from top leadership to be a part of this process. What will help drive that commitment is a strong business case that is less about being a nice thing to do and more about being a smart thing for ensuring that organizations are tapping into the entire rich pool of leadership talent and thinking.

5. Engage Men and Change Their Mindset

As I mentioned earlier, I believe we have unintentionally left men on the sidelines when it comes to advancing women to the senior ranks. Organizations need to find ways—formally and informally—to bring them into this critical initiative. One of the easiest ways is to have men participate in panels, roundtable discussions, or mentoring pods that revolve around women's issues and aspirations. SHAMBAUGH has found this to be a natural way for our clients to engage men with women in a productive two-way dialogue to talk about issues that normally are not put on the table, such as achieving work–personal life integration, managing organizational politics, asking for what you want, and other Sticky Floor issues.

While some of these activities are generally instituted as part of a broader program or initiative, there are some things men can do on their own as senior business leaders. Not too long ago, I coached a male executive on this idea, and while he had some skepticism up front, he elected to host a breakfast for the company's female high-potentials. He later attended a women's global conference and heard firsthand about their aspirations, their challenges, and their different views on important business issues. He later shared with me that this was an extraordinary growth experience for him both personally and professionally.

I encourage you and your organization to engage men to be champions of women and to go out and talk with the top talented women in the company. They can try things as simple as having lunch or coffee with some of the women. Men benefit from this experience first as they start to value the differences in how women show up as leaders and then as they begin to consider how to integrate them into the fabric of the business. You will be amazed how men taking on these roles will create a positive buzz that goes through the organization very quickly and inspires other men to do the same.

Another significant thing organizations can do is to help men recognize the value of their role as a mentor, coach, or sponsor. Many of their strengths are in areas where women can fall short, so organizations need to let men know how their strengths and advice can really make a difference for the women in their organization. It's important to provide men with the tools and strategies that will create a comfort zone for them being a mentor, coach, or sponsor to women. Consider a targeted program that helps men learn about these roles, helps them understand how their strengths and experiences can help women to gain more confidence and competence, and provides them with coaching and mentoring techniques for addressing women's Sticky Floors. Here are some of the key topics that should be included in such a program:

- **The business case for integrated leadership.** Explores how balanced leadership leads to better business results
- **Gender intelligence.** Reviews research regarding gender intelligence and provides an overview of women's Sticky Floors
- **Mentor, coach, and sponsor.** Examines the three different roles and the unique value of each
- **Barriers and obstacles.** Explores biases and assumptions related to women
- **Attributes and attitudes.** Investigates what makes a great mentor, coach, or sponsor

- **Tools and techniques.** Identifies ways to coach women off their Sticky Floors
- **Women and leadership.** Focuses on using Appreciative Leadership with women on your team
- **Women and feedback.** Determines how to have a "difficult conversation" that works for both of you

6. Adopt Best Practices for Advancing Women

An important part of creating and sustaining an Integrated Leadership Model is ensuring that the women in your organization have a deeper awareness of their leadership capabilities, gain the confidence and competence to show up in an authentic way, and take prudent risks for advancing to the senior levels of leadership. Last, it's key that they learn how their unique qualities are an important part of the organization's leadership equation.

It's critical that organizations be proactive not only in identifying potential women leaders, but also in providing them with the right exposure, learning experiences, and work experiences to take their leadership thinking and qualities to their highest potential.

Here are some best practices that SHAMBAUGH recommends for developing and advancing the women in your organization:

- **Tap women in the pipeline early on.** A number of studies indicate that there is a rich pool of talented women in entry, managerial, and emerging leader roles. It's important that organizations reach out to these women early on in their career and be proactive in the conversations and actions they have with them. Why is it important to be proactive? While some women are moving to the executive suite, there are still thousands of women in the leadership pipeline that lose interest in taking their leadership to that next level. This can be due to the competing pressure between work and home life or the organization's cultural obstacles; whatever the reason, it seems that many women limit their ambitions and their career and leadership aspirations as time goes on. This can be a significant issue if a company cannot promote the women it has invested in and more so if it is concerned that these women will leave the company. So the key is to help women gain greater self-awareness and confidence in their skills and to recognize their unique value equation.

- **Initiate two-way conversations regarding their career goals.** Discuss the big picture with a focus on longer-term goals regarding their career and leadership at the company. Give feedback on their leadership strengths and development areas, and then establish a plan that will ensure there is intentional follow-up and ongoing support to forward their career growth, while also being sensitive to their personal life goals and responsive to their specific concerns. It's also critical to encourage them to seek the opportunities that will enable them to advance into senior leadership roles. Support women with a senior mentor or sponsor within the organization who is aligned with their key career goals and is committed to seeing them advance to the next level.

- **Create connections and visibility for them.** Strengthen the connections between these women and the senior executives or key male stakeholders in your organization. Provide opportunities for the exchange of ideas and experiences so that not only do these women feel valued, but they can also begin to explore and validate their concerns and assumptions about the nature and demands of the executive role. Create opportunities for women in your organization to cross-network, share ideas, share challenges and concerns, and cross-mentor each other when appropriate.

- **Be sure each woman has a meaningful development plan.** Put together a targeted plan that includes a customized series of development programs and 360-degree assessment, as well as mentoring and potential sponsorship. It could also include a combination of face-to-face forums, virtual labs for keeping the learning alive, and one-on-one coaching.
- **Ensure these women have excellent coaching.** Provide outstanding one-on-one coaching for women who are on the cusp of advancing to the very senior levels of leadership. Having coached hundreds of women leaders, I know from experience that if a woman has what we refer to as "on-boarding" coaching, it gives them a better platform for success. Coaching at this particular time helps them to gain a better understanding of the context of the new role, the dynamics of the new environment, the new skills important for the job, the key relationships, and so on. For many women, it's all about getting out of their comfort zone; and with coaching and a targeted development plan, they are much more willing to take on more senior roles.
- **Provide targeted learning programs.** While organizations have a wealth of courses available to all employees, programs that address specific needs for women make a tremendous difference. More than 50 percent of the women who attend these programs take on greater responsibility in their organization within 12 months, and many companies use these programs as their key retention strategy for their high-potential women.

7. Create a Culture That Promotes Risk Taking and Flexibility

In order for men or women to advance to senior positions, it's important to create a culture where people are rewarded for taking prudent risks and are not held back if they aren't 100 percent successful in their efforts. We tell people to try new things, but then if they miss the mark, we don't reward them—and sometimes we even punish them! In today's challenging and busy work environment, 80 percent is often good enough. This is especially the case when people take on something that provides them with an opportunity to broaden their skills, expand their knowledge in a particular area, or gain a greater level of confidence in a new arena—all of which helps to prepare them for the next level of leadership. Companies need to be more intentional in how they encourage people to take a risk and how they measure them for doing it. If people take a prudent risk and achieve 80 percent success, then reward them at the 80 percent level versus 100 percent, but be sure to acknowledge them for what they achieved. Encourage them to try new things so that they will be prepared for taking on greater responsibility.

Another aspect of creating the right culture for attracting and retaining your top talent is to foster an environment of flexibility, which allows people to integrate their work with the demands and priorities of their personal life. Be committed to creating flexible programs such as working from home, extending maternity leave, establishing flextime hours, and even instituting sabbaticals to support the well-being of your employees.

A great example of this is CBA's initiative that rewards results over face time. CBA decided to create innovative workspaces for many employees along with business-unit-specific offerings such as a Maternity Leave Register, which allows women on leave to apply for new opportunities. CBA also implemented more traditional flexibility options, such as telecommuting, part-time work, and job share. Because of CBA's strong support for flexibility, the proportion of employees who state they work flexibly (formally and informally) has increased from 35 percent in 2008 to 41 percent in 2011. Of those working flexibly in 2011, 36 percent are men.

To ensure that leaders are held accountable for flexibility and diversity progress, the senior leaders are measured on these things, and specific performance indicators are tied to bonus compensation. These metrics are essential to the success of this effort, and CBA is reaping the benefits already! For example, its representation of women in executive roles increased from 21 percent in 2005 to 30 percent in 2011, and the percentage of women on the board of directors also increased from 20 to 27 percent. From branch manager to CEO, women represent almost 45 percent of leaders in CBA. In addition, women's engagement scores were above Gallup's "world's best-practice levels" in three out of the last four years. That's walking the talk of flexibility!

8. Put the Right Rewards and Incentives in Place

Do you have the right balance of leadership thinking on your team and across the organization? Accountability for internal programs consists of complementary qualitative and quantitative components that ensure the progress of culture change within the organization. Results from the Sodexo's Diversity Index and Balanced Scorecard impacted 10 to 25 percent of bonus compensation for senior executives, depending on their leadership level. In keeping with the organization's long-term focus, this incentive is paid regardless of the company's financial performance for the fiscal year. To gain focus and commitment for your leadership, link key goals to your balanced scorecard. A balanced scorecard has four elements to it: business results, financials, process orientation, and people. Put metrics around the people dimension. This is a leading-edge metric for a company's success. Be sure you are rewarding your managers and leaders for building balance on their teams and for attracting, hiring, and promoting talented women. Build the metrics, monitor the situation, and reward people accordingly!

9. Manage the Talent Pool to Achieve the Right Leadership Balance

I always ask executives how their strategic growth plan maps to their talent management plan. Then I ask how diverse their pool of leadership talent is . . . do they have a balanced leadership team, and are they grooming a diverse group of leaders for the future? If they say, "We have it covered this year," well that's good, but I know that they could be shooting themselves in the foot. Developing talent and building a balanced leadership team doesn't happen overnight. It's an intentional and constant responsibility that every leader should be thinking about every day. Executives who have longer-range, strategic thinking around talent management have been able to attract and keep top talent and develop their capabilities so that those individuals continue to bring greater value to their organizations. However, it's not just about hiring the right talent; it's being mindful about attracting, hiring, and retaining a diverse spectrum of thinking, perspectives, and approaches that will ensure your organization has a balanced leadership approach for decision making, problem solving, and so on.

To have the right balance of leadership, organizations and their leaders need to intentionally manage their talent. The question is, who in the organization ultimately *owns* talent today? If talent management isn't driven by the CEO and the executive team, there's a real problem. What often happens is that it gets delegated to vice presidents and senior vice presidents who are overwhelmed with managing the day-to-day business activities and making sure they meet their quarterly business numbers. I constantly hear from many of them that they don't have time for talent management, because they are too busy driving for results. Or I hear, "I can't take a chance on Liz and let her run this big project because she might screw up and I just can't deal with that right now, so we'll think about her later."

All of senior leadership needs to own and talk about talent. And senior leaders need to call each other on it. Someone needs to say, "John, what's going on with Liz? We saw her as a really bright talent, but I noticed you didn't give her the project lead on this. What's going on with that?" If you're a senior leader, you need to know who your top 50 high-potentials are. When reviewing candidates for senior positions, if you don't see a woman or a minority on the list, you have to push back and say there's something wrong. You have to go back to the members of your talent management team and ask them to bring you a pool of qualified women and diverse men.

I spoke with Robert Gama, vice president of human resources, Worldwide People & Organizational Capabilities at Lenovo, about how Lenovo ensures that its managers are responsible for bringing up diverse talent, whether gender or multicultural. Robert told me:

The reality is that your internal makeup needs to mirror that of your business strategy and external consumer base. For example, at Lenovo, we can see the trend line increasing and the number of technology users who are becoming female and the needs of that population. We want to make sure that we have that understanding and that capability to leverage the women's marketplace.

Wherever you're trying to go with your business, you better make sure that you've got the internal representation so that you understand that market, that need, and the customer buying behaviors. When we look at new hires, we track every year how many were diverse candidates (as defined by men, women, ethnicity). That information feeds into targets that we set internally around our leadership bench. We then take a look at the succession of the bench capacity and bring that into our hiring conversations on a regular basis. For example, if a leader were to leave now, who is his or her bench? Who are those three candidates that can take this person's place? We try to make sure one of those three candidates is diverse, meaning a female. The female candidate may not be *the* choice, but the debate and discussion is there, which creates some visibility and exposure in the discussion that in my opinion is critical and needed to drive that balance we need in leadership representation."

I hope this chapter has helped you to recognize the need for and value of having more women at the executive level and has given you some ideas on how to make this happen. If you are running talent and development in your organization, use these steps as a road map to transform your organization and lead it effectively into the future.

Chapter Summary

- The importance of the organization and its top leadership in developing an Integrated Leadership Model can't be underestimated.
- To create gender-diverse leadership teams, use a systematic approach:
  - Build and communicate the business case that is most relevant and compelling for your organization and link it to your leaders' goals.
  - Create an inclusive corporate culture that encourages and sustains balanced leadership.
  - Build and leverage gender intelligence by raising awareness about biases and the different ways that men and women think, make decisions, negotiate, communicate, and resolve conflicts.
  - Advance talent through proactive sponsorship.
  - Engage men and help them recognize the value of their roles as mentors, coaches, or sponsors for women.
  - Adopt best practices for advancing women.
  - Create a culture that rewards people for taking prudent risks and foster an environment of flexibility that allows people to integrate their work and personal life.
  - Strategically manage the talent pool from the top to achieve the right leadership balance.

Part IV Summary

Companies that implement organizational *best practices* can achieve Integrated Leadership—in our lifetime. Those organizations that lag behind in accepting and embracing the Integrated Leadership proposition, especially at the senior levels, are only going to hurt themselves and their shareholders. I believe that in the future, the best-performing companies will be those that truly embrace the Integrated Leadership Model and are intentional about developing and blending the broader spectrum of gender intelligence. I also believe that smart companies will see the value equation in Integrated Leadership and will be putting more women in senior leadership roles.

Here are a few questions to help you move this idea of Integrated Leadership from conversation to intentional action:

- Do you have a strong business case for Integrated Leadership, and are you incorporating it across the organization?
- Are your recruitment and hiring practices focused on having a balance of men and women in leadership positions?
- Do you hold your leadership team accountable for bringing talented women into the organization, recognizing their potential, and moving them through the leadership pipeline—all the way to the top?
- Are you creating an organizational culture that is aware of the broader gender intelligence and moves people beyond common biases and false assumptions about women in senior leadership positions?
- Where and how are you bringing men into the solution to gain greater Integrated Leadership?

- Do you provide targeted development programs for women leaders, and are you addressing the right things—like the Sticky Floors and sponsorship?
- Do you have the right flexibility and incentives in place to sustain Integrated Leadership throughout your organization?

Conclusion

THE WORLD IS CHANGING, and in doing so, it's impacting our society, our world of business, and our personal lives. As I said at the beginning of this book, it is the perfect storm for our leadership models to change and adapt to the new world in which we are working and living. It's time for a leadership model that reflects the twenty-first century.

I believe that the Integrated Leadership Model will be the catalyst for men and women coming together at the senior level to leverage the broader spectrum of gender intelligence in order for organizations to innovate and engage their way to success—now and in the future. It all comes down to the business case: better balance means better business results!

So are you ready to make this happen—for yourself and for your organization? The world is ready, and I invite you to join in and be the champion for change!

- If you are a man, I invite you to consider how you can leverage your experience and perspectives and be a champion for creating a balanced leadership team in your organization. Expand your role to become a mentor, coach, or sponsor for the talented women in your organization.
- If you are a woman who aspires to senior leadership, know that your natural traits reflect the in-demand attributes for the twenty-first century. I encourage you to show up and tap into these unique gifts. Be open and reach out to men, who

can be helpful mentors and sponsors. Embrace continuous learning, understand your Sticky Floors, and then have the courage to do something about those that may be holding you back from taking a seat at the leadership table.

- If you lead an organization, start moving from conversation to action. Be committed to creating the culture and providing the resources and development necessary to make Integrated Leadership a reality.

Yes, there's no doubt about it. It's time for men and women to leverage their unique strengths and, working together at the top, to lead their organizations to unprecedented levels of success! The question is . . . who will step up and make it happen? I hope it will be you! Wishing you much success in *your* leadership journey now and in the future.

Index

About the Author

Rebecca Shambaugh is an internationally recognized leadership educator, author, speaker, and executive coach with more than 25 years of experience helping organizations and their executives respond to leadership challenges and marketplace opportunities.

As president of SHAMBAUGH, a global leadership development organization, she has coached and worked with Fortune 500 senior executives, providing advice and best practices in the development of existing and future leadership talent, employee engagement, culture transformation, strategic thinking, emotional intelligence, and executive presence. Her clients include such premier organizations as AIG, AT&T, Booz Allen Hamilton, Cisco, Department of the Interior, Dow Chemical, Hilton Worldwide, HP, IBM, KPMG, Johnson & Johnson, Marriott, Oracle, MetLife, Microsoft, Pfizer, and Shell Oil. Prior to starting her own company, she worked for General Motors, Fairchild Industries, and Amax Inc. as a senior executive in the leadership and human resources arena.

In 1995, Rebecca founded Women in Leadership and Learning (WILL), the first executive leadership development program in the country dedicated to the research, advancement, and retention of women. Seventeen years later, WILL programs continue to be an integral part of the advancement strategies of successful female executives.

Rebecca is the author of two books that have been published in six different languages: *Leadership Secrets of Hillary Clinton* (McGraw-Hill, New York, 2010) and *It's Not a Glass Ceiling, It's a Sticky Floor* (McGraw-Hill, New York, 2007). She is a member of the National Press Club and has been featured in numerous prominent publications, including the *New York Times, Washington Post, Huffington Post, Time, USA Today, Fortune, U.S. News & World Report, Pink Magazine, American Executive Magazine,* and *Entrepreneur.*

A highly sought-after speaker, Rebecca has presented across the globe to over 200,000 leaders at conferences and executive forums and within major organizations. Her unconventional and results-focused approach to creating great leaders was showcased on National Public Radio and a PBS telecast to more than 20,000 executives across the United States. She has also appeared on Fox News (New York), *Washington Business* (ABC), and various syndicated radio shows.

Rebecca is committed to working with social-sector organizations and purpose-driven nonprofits. She is the founder and chairman of Young Women Lead, a nonprofit that focuses on the development of the next generation of women leaders. She currently serves on the executive board of the Virginia Women's Center and the Board of Visitors for Marymount University, and she was formerly the chairman of the Northern Virginia Technology Council's Human Resource Advisory Board.

SHAMBAUGH *Leadership*

SHAMBAUGH's mission is to strengthen and sustain the capacity of leaders across the world and provide integrated solutions for the existing and future leadership talent pool. For over 20 years, SHAMBAUGH has built a solid reputation and brand known for its proven level of excellence, business acumen, and experience. SHAMBAUGH specializes in the following areas: leadership development, executive coaching, women's leadership, and organizational effectiveness.

SHAMBAUGH is known for results-driven programs and solutions that focus on critical leadership behaviors and strategies. SHAMBAUGH's innovative and customized programs and solutions have consistently enhanced individual and organizational growth and performance for clients such as IBM, Marriott International, Microsoft, Intelsat, Oracle, Cisco, Booz Allen Hamilton, Ernst & Young, KPMG, Verizon, Dow Chemical, MedImmune, MetLife, Pfizer, the Department of the Interior, and other U.S. government agencies.

You can contact SHAMBAUGH at
http://www.shambaughleadership.com